NINJA CREAMI DELUXE COOKBOOK FOR BEGINNERS

1500-Day Tasty Ice Cream, Ice Cream Mix-In, Shake, Sorbet, And Smoothie Recipes To Make Your Own Mouthwatering Ice Creams At Home

ALICIA D. ELIAS

EDITOR: LYN   INTERIOR DESIGN: FAIZAN

COVER ART: ABR   FOOD STYLIST: JO

Table of Contents

Making ice cream using a Ninja Creami with your family at home can be a fun and enjoyable activity. It can also be a great way to spend quality time together while creating delicious frozen treats that everyone can enjoy.

Making ice cream together can be a fun and bonding experience for your family. It can be a great opportunity to spend quality time together and create memories that you will cherish.

Making ice cream allows you and your family to be creative with flavors and mix-ins. You can experiment with different combinations of ingredients to create unique and delicious ice cream flavors.

Making ice cream can also be a learning opportunity for your family. It can be a chance to learn about food science and how different ingredients interact with each other to create the final product.

Making your own ice cream at home allows you to control the ingredients and make healthier options. You can use natural sweeteners and fresh fruits to create nutritious and delicious desserts.

The Ninja Creami is a popular kitchen appliance that can be used to make a wide variety of frozen treats, including ice cream, sorbet, and frozen yogurt. It is designed to quickly and easily create frozen desserts in minutes, without the need for pre-freezing or churning.

Chapter 1
Basic Guide of Ninja Creami

What is the Ninja Creami?

The Ninja Creami is a kitchen appliance designed to quickly and easily make a variety of frozen treats, including ice cream, sorbet, and frozen yogurt. It uses a unique blending and freezing technology to create frozen desserts in just a few minutes, without the need for pre-freezing or churning. The Ninja Creami has a powerful motor that blends and freezes the ingredients simultaneously, resulting in a smooth and creamy texture. It also allows you to customize your desserts with different flavors and mix-ins. The Ninja Creami comes with various attachments and accessories, including a container, a blade assembly, and a tamper tool, making it a versatile and convenient option for making frozen treats at home.

The Ninja Creami has become increasingly popular in the United States since its introduction to the market. Many people use it to create homemade frozen desserts quickly and easily. The Ninja brand is known for producing high-quality and innovative kitchen appliances, and the Ninja Creami is no exception. Its ability to create frozen treats in just a few minutes without the need for pre-freezing or churning has made it a popular choice for busy individuals and families who want to enjoy homemade desserts. Additionally, the ability to customize desserts with different flavors and mix-ins has made it appealing to those who enjoy experimenting with new recipes and flavors.

Brief History of Ninja Creami Technology

The Ninja Creami technology was developed by SharkNinja, a company that specializes in producing innovative and high-quality household appliances. The technology behind the Ninja Creami was first introduced in 2019 with the launch of the Ninja Foodi Cold & Hot Blender, which was designed to blend and cook ingredients simultaneously.

In 2020, SharkNinja launched the Ninja Creami, which utilized the same technology as the Foodi Cold & Hot Blender, but with a focus on creating frozen desserts. The Ninja Creami was designed to blend and freeze ingredients simultaneously, resulting in a smooth and creamy texture without the need for pre-freezing or churning. This innovative technology was achieved through a combination of a powerful motor, sharp blades, and a cooling element that could rapidly freeze the ingredients.

The Ninja Creami also featured a unique mixing paddle that helped incorporate air into the mixture, resulting in a lighter and fluffier texture. Additionally, the Creami came with various attachments and accessories, including a container, blade assembly, and tamper tool, that allowed for easy and convenient use.

Since its launch, the Ninja Creami has become a popular appliance among those who love frozen desserts and

want to create them easily at home. Its innovative technology has made it possible to make delicious homemade ice cream, sorbet, and frozen yogurt in just a few minutes, without the need for pre-freezing or churning.

Definition and Explanation of the Technology

The Ninja Creami technology is a combination of several advanced techniques that work together to produce frozen desserts quickly and easily. This technology uses a powerful motor, sharp blades, and a cooling element to blend and freeze ingredients simultaneously, resulting in a smooth and creamy texture without the need for pre-freezing or churning.

The Ninja Creami technology is achieved through the following components:

1. Powerful Motor: The Creami's motor is strong enough to blend and freeze the ingredients at the same time, resulting in a creamy texture.
2. Sharp Blades: The blades are designed to quickly and effectively chop and blend the ingredients, resulting in a smooth and even texture.
3. Cooling Element: The Creami has a built-in cooling element that can quickly freeze the ingredients as they are being blended, resulting in a smooth and creamy texture.
4. Mixing Paddle: The Creami also has a unique mixing paddle that helps incorporate air into the mixture, resulting in a lighter and fluffier texture.

The combination of these advanced techniques enables the Ninja Creami to create frozen desserts in just a few minutes, without the need for pre-freezing or churning. This technology is particularly appealing to those who love frozen desserts but want to create them easily and quickly at home.

Features and Benefits of Using the Ninja Creami

There are several features and benefits of using the Ninja Creami to make frozen desserts:
1. Easy to Use: The Ninja Creami is designed to be user-friendly and easy to operate, with intuitive controls and simple assembly. It comes with a user manual that explains how to use the device and includes recipes to get you started. The assembly process is straightforward, and the Creami's parts are easy to attach and detach.
2. Quick and Efficient: The Creami can create frozen desserts in just a few minutes, making it a quick and efficient way to satisfy a sweet tooth. It can make up to 2 quarts of ice cream in just 20 minutes, which is much faster than traditional ice cream makers.
3. No Pre-Freezing or Churning Required: Unlike traditional ice cream makers, the Creami doesn't require pre-

freezing or churning, making it a convenient option for those who want to make frozen desserts without any additional steps. This means that you can make ice cream or frozen yogurt anytime without having to wait for the freezer to freeze the bowl or churn the mixture for a long time.

4.   Customizable: The Creami allows you to customize your desserts with different flavors and mix-ins, giving you the flexibility to experiment with new recipes and create unique combinations. You can add fruits, candies, nuts, chocolate chips, or any other ingredient you like to create your favorite ice cream flavor.

5.   Smooth and Creamy Texture: The Creami's advanced blending and freezing technology results in a smooth and creamy texture that rivals store-bought frozen desserts. The Creami's powerful motor and sharp blades combine with the cooling element to produce a consistent texture without ice crystals, making it feel just like soft-serve ice cream.

6.   Versatile: The Creami can be used to make a variety of frozen desserts, including ice cream, sorbet, and frozen yogurt. This versatility allows you to create a range of different desserts, depending on your preferences or dietary restrictions.

7.   Easy to Clean: The Creami's parts are easy to disassemble and dishwasher safe, making it easy to clean up after use. The device comes with a cleaning brush that helps to clean the blades and mixing paddle effectively. This makes the Creami a low-maintenance appliance that is easy to use and maintain.

Care and Cleaning

Proper care and cleaning are essential to maintain the longevity of your Ninja Creami and ensure it continues to produce delicious frozen desserts. Here are some tips on how to care for and clean your Creami:

1.   Unplug the Creami and allow it to cool before cleaning.
2.   Disassemble the Creami by removing the mixing paddle and the cooling element.
3.   Rinse the mixing paddle and cooling element under running water to remove any residue.
4.   Use a soft brush or sponge to clean the mixing paddle and the inside of the cooling element. Do not use abrasive or sharp objects that can damage the blades.
5.   Wipe the exterior of the Creami with a damp cloth to remove any spills or stains.
6.   Dry all parts thoroughly with a clean cloth or air-dry them before reassembling the Creami.
7.   Store the Creami in a dry and cool place, free from direct sunlight or moisture.
8.   Clean the Creami after every use to prevent the buildup of residue and bacteria.
9.   If the Creami develops any problems, refer to the troubleshooting section of the user manual or contact the manufacturer for assistance.

By following these simple steps, you can ensure that your Ninja Creami stays in top condition and produces delicious frozen desserts every time you use it.

Chapter 2
Time for An Ice Cream Party

Ingredients Matter

One of the great benefits of using a Ninja Creami is the flexibility it provides in terms of ingredients. You can choose from a wide range of ingredients to create your own unique flavor combinations. Here are some examples of ingredients you can use with the Ninja Creami:

1. Dairy: Dairy products like milk, cream, half-and-half, or yogurt provide a creamy base for your frozen desserts. Whole milk and heavy cream will give you the creamiest texture, while low-fat milk or yogurt will result in a lighter texture.
2. Non-dairy alternatives: Non-dairy alternatives like almond milk, coconut milk, or soy milk are great options for those who are lactose intolerant or vegan. They can produce a creamy texture similar to dairy products.
3. Sweeteners: Sweeteners like sugar, honey, or maple syrup are used to give your mixture a sweet taste. You can adjust the amount of sweetener you use depending on your taste preferences.
4. Flavorings: Flavorings like vanilla extract, cocoa powder, or fruit puree are used to give your mixture a unique taste. Vanilla extract is a popular choice for creating a classic vanilla flavor, while cocoa powder is used to make chocolate-flavored frozen desserts. Fruit puree can add a natural fruit flavor to your mixture.
5. Mix-ins: Mix-ins like chopped nuts, chocolate chips, fruit pieces, or candy can be added to your frozen desserts to give them texture and flavor. Chopped nuts can provide a crunchy texture, while fruit pieces can add a natural sweetness.
6. Spices: Spices like cinnamon, nutmeg, or ginger can be added to your mixture to give it a warm and spicy flavor. These spices can also enhance the flavor of other ingredients in your mixture.

Try Different Types of Frozen Treats

Frozen treats are a beloved dessert all over the world, and there are many different types of frozen desserts that you can enjoy. Here's a delicious journey through the different types of frozen treats:

1. Ice Cream: Ice cream is a classic frozen treat that is loved by people of all ages. It is made with a mixture of milk, cream, sugar, and flavorings, and is churned to create a creamy texture. Ice cream can be enjoyed in

many different flavors, such as chocolate, vanilla, strawberry, and many more.

2. Gelato: Gelato is a type of Italian ice cream that is made with milk, cream, sugar, and flavorings. It has a denser and creamier texture than traditional ice cream, and is often served at a slightly warmer temperature than ice cream. Gelato can be enjoyed in many different flavors, such as pistachio, hazelnut, and fruit flavors.

3. Sorbet: Sorbet is a frozen dessert that is made with fruit puree, sugar, and water. It is a dairy-free option that is refreshing and light, and is often served as a palate cleanser between courses of a meal. Sorbet can be enjoyed in many different fruit flavors, such as raspberry, mango, and lemon.

4. Sherbet: Sherbet is a frozen dessert that is similar to sorbet but contains a small amount of dairy, usually in the form of milk or cream. It has a creamy texture and is often served in fruity flavors, such as orange or lime.

5. Frozen Yogurt: Frozen yogurt is a healthier alternative to ice cream that is made with yogurt, milk, sugar, and flavorings. It has a tangy and slightly sour flavor, and is often served with toppings like fresh fruit, granola, or nuts.

6. Popsicles: Popsicles are frozen treats that are made with fruit juice or puree, sugar, and water. They are often served on a stick and come in many different flavors, such as cherry, grape, and orange.

7. Granita: Granita is a semi-frozen dessert that originated in Italy. It is made with sugar, water, and flavorings, and is often served with fresh fruit or whipped cream. Granita has a texture that is somewhere between sorbet and shaved ice.

With so many different types of frozen treats to choose from, there is always something new and delicious to try. Whether you prefer creamy ice cream, tangy frozen yogurt, or refreshing sorbet, there is a frozen dessert out there for everyone.

Fun with Mix-Ins

Mix-ins are a great way to add texture and flavor to your frozen treats. Here are some fun and creative mix-ins that you can try with your Ninja Creami:

1. Chocolate chips: Chocolate chips are a classic mix-in that can be added to almost any flavor of frozen dessert. They add a delicious chocolatey crunch to your frozen treats.

2. Cookie pieces: Crushed up cookies, such as Oreos or chocolate chip cookies, can be added to your frozen dessert to create a fun and flavorful mix-in.

3. Candy pieces: Chopped up candy, such as M&Ms or Reese's Pieces, can be added to your frozen dessert for a fun and colorful mix-in.

4. Fruit pieces: Chopped up fresh fruit, such as strawberries or bananas, can be added to your frozen dessert to add a natural sweetness and texture.

5. Nuts: Chopped nuts, such as almonds or pecans, can be added to your frozen dessert for a crunchy texture and nutty flavor.

6. Cereal: Crushed up cereal, such as Fruity Pebbles or Cinnamon Toast Crunch, can be added to your frozen dessert to create a unique and flavorful mix-in.

7. Marshmallows: Mini marshmallows can be added to your frozen dessert for a fun and sweet mix-in.

8. Coconut flakes: Shredded coconut can be added to your frozen dessert to add a tropical flavor and texture.

What Not to Mix In

While there are many delicious mix-ins that you can add to your frozen treats, there are also some ingredients that you should avoid mixing in. Here are some examples of what not to mix in:

1. Liquids: Avoid adding liquids, such as syrups or juices, directly to your frozen dessert mixture. This can cause the mixture to become too thin and may affect the texture and consistency of your frozen treat.

2. Hard candies: Hard candies can be difficult to mix into your frozen dessert mixture and may not dissolve fully, leaving hard pieces in your frozen treat.

3. Fresh herbs or spices: While fresh herbs and spices can add unique and interesting flavors to your cooking, they may not mix well with frozen treats and can affect the overall taste and texture.

4. Meat or seafood: Meat and seafood should not be added to your frozen desserts. These ingredients do not mix well with sweet flavors and may also pose a food safety risk if not cooked properly.

5. Garlic or onions: Garlic and onions are strong and savory flavors that do not mix well with sweet flavors. They can also affect the overall taste and aroma of your frozen treat.

Remember to always use caution and common sense when choosing mix-ins for your frozen treats. Stick to ingredients that complement the flavors of your frozen dessert and avoid adding anything that may negatively affect the texture or taste.

Q&As

How long does it take to make frozen treats with the Ninja Creami?
The amount of time it takes to make frozen treats with the Ninja Creami varies depending on the recipe and ingredients used, but most frozen treats can be made in just a few minutes.

Is the Ninja Creami loud when in use?
The Ninja Creami is a powerful machine, so it can be somewhat loud when in use. However, it is not excessively loud and is comparable to other kitchen appliances such as blenders or food processors.

How big is the Ninja Creami?
The Ninja Creami has a compact design and measures approximately 9 inches by 6 inches. It can easily fit on most kitchen counters or be stored away in a cabinet when not in use.

Does the Ninja Creami require any pre-freezing of ingredients or the machine itself?
No, the Ninja Creami does not require any pre-freezing of ingredients or the machine itself. Simply add your ingredients to the mixing bowl and turn on the machine to start making your frozen treats.

Can the Ninja Creami make other types of desserts besides frozen treats?
While the Ninja Creami is primarily designed for making frozen treats, it can also be used to create other desserts such as whipped cream, mousse, and frosting.

Can the Ninja Creami be used with young children?
The Ninja Creami is generally safe for use with children, but it is recommended that adults supervise children while using the machine.

Is the Ninja Creami machine dishwasher safe?
No, the Ninja Creami machine itself is not dishwasher safe. Only the removable mixing bowl, blade, and lid are dishwasher safe. The machine can be wiped down with a damp cloth.

Chapter 3
Ice Cream Recipes

Date, Rum, & Pecan Ice Cream

Prep time: 5 minutes | Cook time: 5 minutes| Serves 2-4

- 9 frozen bananas, peeled
- 12 frozen dates, pitted
- 1/2 cup Greek yogurt, vanilla flavored
- 2 tablespoons sugar-free maple syrup
- 3 tablespoons cup spiced rum
- 1 cup pecans, toasted and coarsely chopped
- Pinch of pink Himalayan salt

1. Place a large mixing bowl under the Yonanas chute and push the bananas and dates through.
2. Mix in yogurt, maple syrup, salt and spiced rum until smooth.
3. Fold in chopped pecans.
4. Serve in individual bowls, and freeze leftover soft-serve in an airtight container.

Chocolate Malted Whopper Ice Cream

Prep time: 5 minutes | Cook time: 5 minutes| Serves 3-5

- 10 frozen bananas, peeled
- 1 cup coconut cream, chilled
- 1 tablespoon honey
- 1 teaspoon vanilla
- 1/2 cup Whoppers or chocolate covered malted milk balls

1. Place a mixing bowl under the Yonanas chute and push the bananas through.
2. Add coconut cream, honey and vanilla extract to the mixing bowl.
3. Blend until smooth.
4. Fold in whoppers, and spoon into individual servings.

Frozen Mudslide

Prep time: 5 minutes | Freeze time: 24 hours | Serves 2

- 2 cups ice cubes
- ½ cup store-bought vanilla ice cream
- 6 tablespoons espresso vodka
- 6 tablespoons coffee-flavored liqueur
- 6 tablespoons Irish cream–flavored liqueur

1. Combine the ice, ice cream, vodka, and liqueurs in a blender. Blend on high until smooth.
2. Pour the base into a clean CREAMi Pint. Place the storage lid on the container and freeze for 24 hours.
3. Remove the pint from the freezer and take off the lid. Place the pint in the outer bowl of your Ninja® CREAMi™, install the Creamerizer™ Paddle in the outer bowl lid, and lock the lid assembly onto the outer bowl. Place the bowl assembly on the motor base, and twist the handle to the right to raise the platform and lock it in place. Select the Milkshake function.
4. Once the machine has finished processing, remove the milkshake from the pint. Serve immediately.

Cinnamon Cream Cheese Ice Cream

Prep time: 5 minutes | Cook time: 25 minutes | Serves 4-5

- 12 frozen bananas, peeled
- 8 ounces Neufchatel cheese, softened (alternatively Greek Yogurt Cream Cheese is a great cream cheese substitute)
- 1/4 cup Greek yogurt, vanilla flavored
- 1 tablespoon honey
- 1 1/2 teaspoons cinnamon
- 1/4 cup brown sugar substitute
- 1/3 cup water
- 2 tablespoons cornstarch
- 2 tablespoons unsalted butter

1. Set the Neufchatel cheese out on the counter to come to room temperature for at least 8 hours.
2. Cook up the cinnamon sauce by combining the brown sugar, water, butter, cornstarch, and a 1/2 teaspoon cinnamon over medium heat.
3. Constantly stirring, cook the mixture until the butter has melted and it begins to thicken.
4. Remove from heat and transfer to a mixing bowl; refrigerate until ready to serve.
5. Whip the cheese, using an electric mixer, in a large mixing bowl until it is a smooth, creamy texture.
6. Place the mixing bowl under the Yonanas chute.
7. Push frozen bananas through the Yonanas chute.
8. Add yogurt, honey and 1 teaspoon cinnamon to the mixing bowl.
9. Mix together until smooth and serve.

Lemongrass Ginger Coconut Ice Cream

Prep time: 5 minutes | Cook time: 5 minutes| Serves 3

- 2 cups frozen coconut meat
- 2 stalks of frozen lemongrass, cut into slices
- 1 tablespoon fresh ginger, grated
- 1 cup coconut cream, chilled
- 1 tablespoon honey

1. Place a mixing bowl under the Yonanas chute and push the coconut and lemongrass through.
2. Add grated ginger, coconut cream and honey to the mixing bowl.
3. Blend until smooth.
4. Spoon into single servings.

Peanut Butter and Jelly Ice Cream

Prep time: 1 hour 5 minutes | Cook time: 5 minutes| Serves 3-5

- 10 frozen bananas, peeled
- 1/2 cup soy yogurt, vanilla flavored
- 3 tablespoons natural peanut butter, no sugar added
- 1/4 cup strawberry or red currant preserves

1. Place the mixing bowl under the Yonanas chute and push the bananas through the chute.
2. Add yogurt and peanut butter to the mixing bowl.
3. Mix together until smooth.
4. Fold preserves into the ice cream.
5. Scoop into individual bowls and top with your favorite treat.

Guinness Milk Chocolate Ice Cream

Prep time: 5 minutes | Cook time: 5 minutes| Serves 4

- 12 frozen bananas, peeled
- 1 cup Greek yogurt, vanilla flavored
- 3 tablespoons cocoa powder
- 1 tablespoon brown sugar substitute
- 1/3 cup Guinness Stout

1. Whip yogurt, cocoa powder and brown sugar substitute in a mixing bowl until smooth.
2. Refrigerate for 1 hour to set.
3. Place a large mixing bowl under the Yonanas chute and push the bananas through.
4. Fold in yogurt, then Guinness until smooth.
5. Serve in individual bowls, and freeze leftover soft-serve in an airtight container.

Orange Ice Cream with Dark Chocolate Chip

Prep time: 1 hour 5 minutes | Cook time: 5 minutes| Serves 3-5

- 9 frozen bananas, peeled
- 1 cup frozen oranges, peeled and seeded
- 1/2 cup Greek yogurt, vanilla flavored
- 3 teaspoons cocoa powder
- 3 tablespoons 85% dark cacao bar, chopped

1. Mix the cocoa powder into the Greek yogurt and chill in the refrigerator for 1 hour.
2. Place a mixing bowl under the Yonanas chute.
3. Push the bananas and oranges through.
4. Add the chocolate yogurt and mix until well-blended.
5. Fold in the dark chocolate chunks.
6. Scoop into a cone or bowl.
7. Freeze leftovers in an airtight container.

Raspberry Extract Ice Cream

Prep time: 5 minutes | Cook time: 24 hours 10 minutes| Serves 4

- 1 cup whole milk
- ¾ cup heavy whipped cream
- ½ teaspoon raspberry extract
- ¼ teaspoon lemon extract
- ½ teaspoon vanilla extract
- 4 drops blue food coloring
- 3 tablespoons granulated sugar

1. Beat all the ingredients in a bowl until combined.
2. Transfer the mixture to an empty Ninja CREAMi Pint.
3. Cover the container with the lid and freeze for 24 hours.
4. After 24 hours, remove the lid and place the pint into the outer bowl of the Ninja CREAMi.
5. Install the Creamerizer Paddle onto the lid of the outer bowl.
6. Rotate the lid clockwise to lock. Turn the unit on.
7. Press the ICE CREAM button.
8. When the program is complete, turn the outer bowl and release it from the unit.
9. Serve in bowls.

Tahini and Lemon Curd Ice Cream

Prep time: 5 minutes | Cook time: 5 minutes| Serves 4

- 12 frozen bananas, peeled
- 1/2 cup tahini paste
- 2 teaspoons pure vanilla extract
- 3 tablespoons lemon curd
- 1 teaspoon honey

1. Place a mixing bowl under the Yonanas chute and push the bananas through.
2. Add tahini, vanilla extract, lemon curd and honey to the mixing bowl.
3. Blend until smooth.
4. Spoon into individual bowls and freeze leftover soft-serve in an airtight container.

Coconut Ice cream Of Togetherness

Prep Time: 10 minutes | Cook time: 24 Hours 25 Minutes | Serves 2

- ½ cup sweetened flaked coconut
- ¾ cup heavy cream
- 7 ounces cream of coconut
- ½ cup milk

1. In a food processor or blender, combine the milk and coconut cream and thoroughly mix.
2. Combine the heavy cream and flaked coconut in a mixing bowl, and then add to the milk-cream mixture. Combine well.
3. Pour the mixture into an empty ninja CREAMi Pint container and freeze for 24 hours.
4. After 24 hours, remove the Pint from the freezer. Remove the lid.
5. Place the Ninja CREAMi Pint into the outer bowl. Next, place the outer bowl with the Pint into the ninja CREAMi machine and turn until the outer bowl locks into place. Then, push the ICE CREAM button.
6. Once the ICE CREAM function has ended, turn the outer bowl and release it from the ninja CREAMi machine.

Lavender Cookies And Cream Delight

Prep Time: 10 minutes | Cook time: 24 hours | Serves 2

- ½ cup heavy cream
- ½ tablespoon dried lavender
- ½ cup whole milk
- ¼ cup sweetened condensed milk
- 2 drops purple food coloring
- ¼ cup crushed chocolate wafer cookies

1. Whisk together the heavy cream, lavender, and salt in a medium saucepan.
2. Steep the mixture for 10 minutes over low heat, stirring every 2 minutes to prevent bubbling.
3. Using a fine-mesh strainer, drain the lavender from the heavy cream into a large mixing basin. Discard the lavender.
4. Combine the milk, sweetened condensed milk, and purple food coloring in a large mixing bowl. Whisk until the mixture is completely smooth.
5. Pour the base into an empty CREAMi Pint. Place the Pint into an ice bath. Once cooled, place the storage lid on the Pint and freeze for 24 hours.
6. Remove the Pint from the freezer and remove its lid. Place Pint in outer bowl, install Creamerizer Paddle in outer bowl lid, and lock the lid assembly onto the outer bowl. Select ICE CREAM.
7. When the process is done, create a 1 Vfe-inch wide hole that reaches the bottom of the Pint with a spoon. It's okay if your treat exceeds the max fill line. Add crushed wafer cookies to the hole and process again using the MIX-IN program.
8. When processing is complete, remove ice cream from Pint and serve immediately, topped with extra crumbled wafers if desired.

Vanilla Flavored Ice Cream Chocolate Chips

Prep Time: 10 minutes | **Cook time:** 24 Hours And 5 Minutes | Serves 2

- 1 tablespoons cream cheese, soft
- 1/3 cup granulated sugar
- 1 teaspoon vanilla extract
- ¼ cup heavy cream
- 1 cup whole milk
- ¼ cup mini chocolate chips

1. In a large microwave-safe bowl, microwave the cream cheese for 10 seconds. Blend in the sugar and vanilla extract with a rubber spatula until the mixture resembles frosting, about 60 seconds.
2. Whisk in the heavy cream and milk gradually until the mixture is smooth and the sugar has dissolved.
3. Fill an empty CREAMi Pint with the base. Freeze for 24 hours with the storage lid on the Pint.
4. Remove the lid from the Pint and take it out of the freezer. Place the Pint in the outer bowl, attach the Creamerizer Paddle to the lid of the outer bowl, and secure the lid assembly. ICE CREAM is the option to choose.
5. Create a 1 Vfe-inch wide hole in the bottom of the Pint with a spoon. It's fine for your treat to press above the max fill line during this process. Fill the hole in the Pint with chocolate chips and process again with the MIX-IN program.
6. Remove the ice cream from the Pint once the processing is finished.

Cherry-Chocolate Chunk Ice Cream

Prep time: 5 minutes | **Cook time:** 24 hours 10 minutes | Serves 4

- 1 (6 ounces) packet frozen sweet cherries
- ¾ cup heavy cream
- 1 (7 ounces) can sweetened condensed milk
- ½ cup milk
- 1 teaspoon vanilla extract
- 1 (2 ounces) bar semisweet baking chocolate, broken into small chunks

1. Combine the heavy cream, sweetened condensed milk, milk, and vanilla extract in a mixing bowl.
2. Pour the ice cream mixture into an empty ninja CREAMi Pint container, add the chopped cherries and chocolate chunks, and freeze for 24 hours.
3. After 24 hours, remove the Pint from the freezer. Remove the lid.
4. Place the Ninja CREAMi Pint into the outer bowl. Place the outer bowl with the Pint in it into the ninja CREAMi machine and turn until the outer bowl locks into place. Push the ICE CREAM button.
5. Once the ICE CREAM function has ended, turn the outer bowl and release it from the ninja CREAMi machine.

Creamy Caramel Macchiato Coffee Ice Cream

Prep time: 5 minutes | Cook time: 24 hours 10 minutes | Serves 6

- 1 cup heavy whipping cream
- ½ cup sweetened condensed milk
- ¼ cup coffee-mate caramel macchiato flavored creamer (liquid creamer)
- 1 teaspoon instant coffee granules
- Caramel syrup (for drizzling)

1. Combine all ingredients (except the syrup) in a big mixing bowl of a stand mixer or a large mixing dish.
2. Whip the heavy cream mixture with an electric mixer until firm peaks form (to prevent massive splattering, start at a slower speed, and as the cream thickens, increase the speed). Make sure the whip cream mixture isn't overmixed or "broken."
3. Pour the mixture into an empty ninja CREAMi Pint container and freeze for 24 hours.
4. After 24 hours, remove the Pint from the freezer. Remove the lid.
5. Place the Ninja CREAMi Pint into the outer bowl. Place the outer bowl with the Pint in it into the ninja CREAMi machine and turn until the outer bowl locks into place. Push the ICE CREAM button.
6. Once the ICE CREAM function has ended, turn the outer bowl and release it from the ninja CREAMi machine.

Raspberry White Truffle Ice Cream

Prep time: 5 minutes | Cook time: 24 hours 5 minutes | Serves 1

ICE CREAM BASE:
- 1 tablespoon cream cheese (room temperature)
- ⅓ cup sugar
- 1 tablespoon raspberry preserves
- ¾ cup heavy whipping cream
- 1 cup milk
- ¼ cup raspberries (cut in half)
- Mix-ins:(optional)
- ¼ cup raspberries (cut in half)
- 3 white chocolate truffles (cut in quarters)

1. In a mixing dish, combine the cream cheese, sugar, and raspberry preserves. Using a whisk, blend all ingredients until they are thoroughly mixed and the sugar begins to dissolve.
2. Combine the heavy whipping cream and milk in a mixing bowl. Whisk until all of the ingredients are thoroughly blended. Because the raspberry preserves mixture is fairly thick, this may take a minute or two.
3. Half of the raspberries, cut in half, should be added. Depending on the size, this should yield 6 to 8 raspberries.
4. Once all ingredients have been added (except the mix-ins), pour into an empty ninja CREAMi Pint container and freeze for 24 hours.
5. After 24 hours, remove the Pint from the freezer. Remove the lid.
6. Place the Ninja CREAMi Pint into the outer bowl. Place the outer bowl with the Pint in it into the ninja CREAMi machine and turn until the outer bowl locks into place. Push the ICE CREAM button. During the ICE CREAM function, the ice cream will mix together and become very creamy.
7. Once the ICE CREAM function has ended, turn the outer bowl and release it from the ninja CREAMi machine.
8. Make a hole in the center of the ice cream with a spoon that runs from top to bottom. The mix-ins will be placed in this hole. Add the ¼ cup of raspberries and 3 white chocolate truffles to the mix. Make sure the raspberries are cut in half, and the truffles are sliced into quarters. Because these mix-ins will not be broken down into smaller bits during the mixing process, you'll want to make sure they're in little chunks.
9. Place the outer bowl with the Pint back into the ninja CREAMi machine and lock it into place. Choose the MIX-IN function.
10. Once the Ninja CREAMi completes the MIX-IN cycle, remove the outer bowl from the machine.
11. Your ice cream is ready to eat! Enjoy!

Blackberry Ice Cream

Prep time: 5 minutes | Cook time: 24 hours 10 minutes| Serves 2

- ½ pint fresh blackberries
- ¼ cup white sugar
- ½ teaspoon lemon zest
- 1 cup heavy cream
- ⅓ cup whole milk
- 1 teaspoon vanilla extract

1. Puree the blackberries, sugar, and lemon zest in a blender.
2. Put the purée in a mixing bowl after straining the seeds through a fine-mesh sieve.
3. Combine the cream, milk, and vanilla extract in a mixing bowl. Mix for about 30 seconds or until the mixture is whipped. Add to the purée and mix well.
4. Pour the mixture into an empty ninja CREAMi Pint container and freeze for 24 hours.
5. After 24 hours, remove the Pint from the freezer. Remove the lid.
6. Place the Ninja CREAMi Pint into the outer bowl. Place the outer bowl with the Pint in it into the ninja CREAMi machine and turn until the outer bowl locks into place. Push the ICE CREAM button.
7. Once the ICE CREAM function has ended, turn the outer bowl and release it from the ninja CREAMi machine.

Cinnamon Red Hot Ice Cream

Prep time: 5 minutes | Cook time: 24 hours 10 minutes| Serves 4

- 2 cups heavy whipping cream, divided
- 1 egg yolk
- 1 cup half-and-half
- ½ cup Red Hot candies

1. In a mixing bowl, whisk together 1 cup of cream and the egg yolks until smooth.
2. In another large bowl, combine the half-and-half, 1 cup cream, and Red Hot candies. Whisk with a wooden spoon until the candies dissolve, about 5 to 10 minutes.
3. Pour the cream-egg mixture into the candy mixture and stir to incorporate.
4. Pour the mixture into an empty ninja CREAMi Pint container and freeze for 24 hours.
5. After 24 hours, remove the Pint from the freezer. Remove the lid.
6. Place the Ninja CREAMi Pint into the outer bowl. Place the outer bowl with the Pint in it into the ninja CREAMi machine and turn until the outer bowl locks into place. Push the ICE CREAM button.
7. Once the ICE CREAM function has ended, turn the outer bowl and release it from the ninja CREAMi machine.

Pumpkin Gingersnap Ice Cream

Prep time: 5 minutes | Cook time: 24 hours 15 minutes| Serves 4

- 1 cup heavy whipping cream
- ½ tablespoon vanilla extract
- ½ teaspoon ground cinnamon
- ½ teaspoon ground ginger
- ½ cup solid-pack pumpkin
- 1 (7 ounces) can Eagle Brand sweetened condensed milk
- ½ cup crushed gingersnap cookies

1. In a large mixing bowl, beat the heavy whipping cream, vanilla extract, cinnamon, and ginger with an electric mixer on medium speed until stiff peaks form.
2. Combine the pumpkin and sweetened condensed milk in a mixing bowl.
3. Add the crushed gingersnap cookies to the pumpkin mixture and stir well.
4. Pour the mixture into an empty ninja CREAMi Pint container and freeze for 24 hours.
5. After 24 hours, remove the Pint from the freezer. Remove the lid.
6. Place the Ninja CREAMi Pint into the outer bowl. Place the outer bowl with the Pint in it into the ninja CREAMi machine and turn until the outer bowl locks into place. Push the ICE CREAM button.
7. Once the ICE CREAM function has ended, turn the outer bowl and release it from the ninja CREAMi machine.

Fruity Extract Ice Cream

Prep time: 5 minutes | Cook time: 24 hours 10 minutes| Serves 4

- 1 cup whole milk
- ¾ cup heavy cream
- 2 tablespoons monk fruit sweetener with Erythritol
- 2 tablespoons agave nectar
- ½ teaspoon raspberry extract
- ½ teaspoon vanilla extract
- ¼ teaspoon lemon extract
- 5-6 drops blue food coloring

1. In a bowl, add all ingredients and eat until well combined.
2. Transfer the mixture into an empty Ninja CREAMi pint container.
3. Cover the container with storage lid and freeze for 24 hours.
4. After 24 hours, remove the lid from container and arrange into the Outer Bowl of Ninja CREAMi.
5. Install the Creamerizer Paddle onto the lid of outer bowl.
6. Then rotate the lid clockwise to lock.
7. Press Power button to turn on the unit.
8. Then press Ice Cream button.
9. When the program is completed, turn the Outer Bowl and release it from the machine.
10. Transfer the ice cream into serving bowls and serve immediately.

Chocolate Brownie Ice Cream
Prep time: 5 minutes | Cook time: 3 minutes | Serves 4

- 1 tablespoon cream cheese, softened
- ⅓ cup granulated sugar
- 1 teaspoon vanilla extract
- 2 tablespoons cocoa powder
- 1 cup whole milk
- ¾ cup heavy cream
- 2 tablespoons mini chocolate chips
- 2 tablespoons brownie chunks

1. In a large microwave-safe bowl, add the cream cheese and microwave on High for about ten seconds.
2. Remove from the microwave and stir until smooth.
3. Add the sugar and almond extract and with a wire whisk, beat until the mixture looks like frosting.
4. Slowly add the milk and heavy cream and beat until well combined.
5. Transfer the mixture into an empty Ninja CREAMi pint container.
6. Cover the container with storage lid and freeze for 24 hours.
7. After 24 hours, remove the lid from container and arrange into the Outer Bowl of Ninja CREAMi.
8. Install the Creamerizer Paddle onto the lid of Outer Bowl.
9. Then rotate the lid clockwise to lock.
10. Press Power button to turn on the unit.
11. Then press Ice Cream button.
12. When the program is completed, with a spoon, create a 1½-inch wide hole in the center that reaches the bottom of the pint container.
13. Add the chocolate chunks and brownie pieces into the hole and press Mix-In button. 14. When the program is completed, turn the Outer Bowl and release it from the machine.
14. Transfer the ice cream into serving bowls and serve immediately.

Coffee And Cookies Ice Cream
Prep time: 5 minutes | Cook time: 3 minutes | Serves 4

- 1 tablespoon cream cheese, at room temperature
- ⅓ cup granulated sugar
- 1 teaspoon vanilla extract
- 1 tablespoon instant espresso
- ¾ cup heavy (whipping) cream
- 1 cup whole milk
- ¼ cup crushed chocolate sandwich cookies

1. In a large bowl, whisk together the cream cheese, sugar, and vanilla for about 1 minute, until the mixture looks like frosting.
2. Slowly whisk in the instant espresso, heavy cream, and milk until fully combined.
3. Pour the base into a clean CREAMi Pint. Place the lid on the container and freeze for 24 hours.
4. Remove the pint from the freezer and take off the lid. Place the pint in the outer bowl of your Ninja CREAMi, install the Creamerizer Paddle in the outer bowl lid, and lock the lid assembly onto the outer bowl. Place the bowl assembly on the motor base, and twist the handle to the right to raise the platform and lock it in place. Select the Ice Cream function.
5. Once the machine has finished processing, remove the lid from the pint container. With a spoon, create a 1½-inch-wide hole that reaches the bottom of the pint. Add the crushed cookies to the hole, replace the lid, and select the Mix-In function.
6. Once the machine has finished processing, remove the ice cream from the pint. Serve immediately.

Carrot Ice Cream

Prep time: 5 minutes | Cook time: 1 minutes | Serves 2

- 1 cup heavy cream
- ½ cup carrot juice
- ⅓ cup light brown sugar
- 2 tablespoons cream cheese frosting
- 1 teaspoon vanilla extract
- 1 teaspoon ground cinnamon

1. In a bowl, add all ingredients and beat until well combined.
2. Transfer the mixture into an empty Ninja CREAMi pint container.
3. Cover the container with the storage lid and freeze for 24 hours.
4. After 24 hours, remove the lid from container and arrange into the outer bowl of Ninja CREAMi.
5. Install the "Creamerizer Paddle" onto the lid of outer bowl.
6. Then rotate the lid clockwise to lock.
7. Press "Power" button to turn on the unit.
8. Then press "ICE CREAM" button.
9. When the program is completed, turn the outer bowl and release it from the machine. 10. Transfer the ice cream into serving bowls and serve immediately.

Fruity Carrot Ice Cream

Prep time: 5 minutes | Cook time: 5 minutes | Serves 4

- ¾ cup heavy cream
- ½ cup milk
- ⅓ cup orange juice
- ¾ cup sugar
- ¼ cup frozen carrots
- ¼ cup pineapple chunks

1. In a bowl, add the heavy cream, milk, orange juice and sugar and beat until well combined.
2. In an empty Ninja CREAMi pint container, place the carrots and pineapple chunks and top with milk mixture.
3. Cover the container with the storage lid and freeze for 24 hours.
4. After 24 hours, remove the lid from container and arrange into the outer bowl of Ninja CREAMi.
5. Install the "Creamerizer Paddle" onto the lid of outer bowl.
6. Then rotate the lid clockwise to lock.
7. Press "Power" button to turn on the unit.
8. Then press "ICE CREAM" button.
9. When the program is completed, turn the outer bowl and release it from the machine. 10. Transfer the ice cream into serving bowls and serve immediately.

Strawberry Ice Cream

Prep time: 5 minutes | Cook time: 5 minutes | Serves 4

- ¼ cup sugar
- 1 tablespoon cream cheese, softened
- 1 teaspoon vanilla bean paste
- 1 cup milk
- ¾ cup heavy whipping cream
- 6 medium fresh strawberries, hulled and quartered

1. In a bowl, add the sugar, cream cheese, vanilla bean paste and with a wire whisk, mix until well combined.
2. Add in the milk and heavy whipping cream and beat until well combined.
3. Transfer the mixture into an empty Ninja CREAMi pint container.
4. Add the strawberry pieces and stir to combine.
5. Cover the container with storage lid and freeze for 24 hours.
6. After 24 hours, remove the lid from container and arrange into the Outer Bowl of Ninja CREAMi.
7. Install the Creamerizer Paddle onto the lid of Outer Bowl.
8. Then rotate the lid clockwise to lock.
9. Press Power button to turn on the unit.
10. Then press Ice Cream button.
11. When the program is completed, turn the Outer Bowl and release it from the machine.
12. Transfer the ice cream into serving bowls and serve immediately.

Lime-Basil Sorbet

Prep time: 5 minutes | Cook time: 5 minutes| Serves 4

- 6 frozen bananas, peeled
- 1/2 cup freshly-squeezed lime juice
- 2 tablespoons lime zest
- 3 tablespoons fresh basil, chopped
- Sprig of fresh basil to garnish for parties

1. Place a large mixing bowl under the Yonanas chute.
2. Push the frozen bananas through the chute.
3. Add lime juice, zest and basil to the mixing bowl.
4. Mix until well-blended.
5. Spoon into individual bowls.
6. Freeze leftovers in an airtight container.

Zucchini Lemon Sorbet

Prep time: 5 minutes | Cook time: 5 minutes| Serves 4

- 3 frozen bananas, peeled
- 2 frozen zucchinis, peeled
- 1/4 cup lemon juice
- 1 tablespoon lemon zest

1. Place a large mixing bowl under the Yonanas chute.
2. Push the frozen bananas through the chute.
3. Push the zucchini through the chute.
4. Add the lemon juice and zest to the mixing bowl.
5. Mix until well-blended.
6. Spoon into individual bowls, and freeze leftovers in an airtight container.

Yonanas Sorbet with Rose and Pistachio

Prep time: 5 minutes | Cook time: 5 minutes| Serves 2-4

- 6 frozen bananas, peeled
- 1/4 cup Greek yogurt, vanilla flavored
- 1 tablespoon honey
- 1/2 teaspoon rose water
- 1/2 cup pistachios, chopped

1. Place a mixing bowl under the Yonanas chute and push the bananas through.
2. Add yogurt, honey and rose water to the mixing bowl.
3. Blend until smooth.
4. Spoon into individual bowls, and top each serving with a generous portion of chopped pistachios.
5. Freeze leftover soft-serve in an airtight container.

Raspberry Campari Sorbet

Prep time: 5 minutes | Cook time: 5 minutes| Serves 2-4

- 5 cups frozen raspberries
- 2 tablespoons honey
- 3 tablespoons Campari
- 1 teaspoon fresh-squeezed orange juice
- 1/2 teaspoon fresh orange zest
- 1/4 teaspoon kosher salt
- 1/2 teaspoon fresh lemon juice

1. Place a large mixing bowl under the Yonanas chute.
2. Push the frozen raspberries through the chute.
3. Add honey, Campari, orange juice & zest, lemon juice, and salt to the mixing bowl.
4. Mix until well-blended.
5. Spoon into individual bowls.
6. Freeze leftovers in an airtight container.

Oatmeal Gelato

Prep time:1 hour |Freeze Time:24 hours | Serves 4

- 2 oz. instant oatmeal
- 1 cup hot water
- 1 tablespoon heavy cream powder
- 2 tablespoons yogurt

1. Add the oatmeal to a bowl.
2. Cover with hot water.
3. Let sit for 15 minutes.
4. Transfer oatmeal to your Ninja Creami pint container.
5. Stir in the rest of the ingredients.
6. Freeze for 24 hours.
7. Place in the machine.
8. Choose the Gelato function.

Pumpkin Pie Gelato

Prep time:10 minutes |Freeze Time:24 hours | Serves 4

- 1 ¾ cups milk
- ½ cup pumpkin puree
- ¼ teaspoon allspice
- ½ teaspoon cinnamon
- ¼ cup granulated sugar
- Pinch salt

1. Add all the ingredients to a pan over medium heat.
2. Cook while stirring for 5 minutes.
3. Pour mixture into the Ninja Creami pint container.
4. Freeze for 24 hours.
5. Transfer container to the machine.
6. Press the Gelato function.

Black Cherry Gelato

Prep time:40 minutes |Freeze Time:24 hours | Serves 1 pint

- 4 egg yolks
- 5 tablespoons granulated sugar
- 1 tablespoon corn syrup
- 1 cup heavy cream
- ⅓ cup milk
- 1 teaspoon almond extract
- 1 cup black cherries, sliced

1. Add the egg yolks, sugar and corn syrup to a saucepan.
2. Mix well.
3. Stir in the heavy cream, almond extract and milk.
4. Place the pan over medium heat.
5. Cook until temperature has reached 165 degrees F.
6. Strain the mixture into the Ninja Creami pint container.
7. Freeze for 24 hours.
8. Place in the machine.
9. Press the Gelato function.

Raspberry and Redcurrant Sorbet

Prep time: 5 minutes | Cook time: 5 minutes| Serves 2-4

- 5 cups frozen raspberries
- 2 cups frozen redcurrants, destemmed

1. Place a large mixing bowl under the Yonanas chute and push the raspberries and redcurrants through.
2. Stir until smooth to blend the flavors.
3. Spoon into individual bowls and freeze leftovers in an airtight container.

Mojito Sorbet

Prep Time: 10 minutes | Cook time: 24 Hours 5 Minutes | Serves 2

- ½ cup squeezed lime juice
- 1 teaspoon lime zest, grated
- ½ cup mint leaves, packed
- ½ cup white sugar
- ½ cup water
- ¾ cup citrus-flavored water
- 1 tablespoon rum

1. Add all ingredients to a bowl and mix until the sugar is dissolved. Pour into the ninja CREAMi Pint container and freeze on a level surface in a cold freezer for a full 24 hours.
2. After 24 hours, remove the Pint from the freezer. Remove the lid.
3. Place the Ninja CREAMi Pint into the outer bowl. Place the outer bowl with the Pint into the ninja CREAMi machine and turn until the outer bowl locks into place. Push the SORBET button. During the SORBET function, the sorbet will mix together and become very creamy. This should take approximately 2 minutes.
4. Once the SORBET function has ended, turn the outer bowl and release it from the ninja CREAMi machine.
5. Your sorbet is ready to eat! Enjoy!

Maple Gelato

Prep time:10 minutes | Freeze Time:24 hours | Serves 4

- 1 tablespoon maple syrup
- 1 teaspoon maple extract
- 4 egg yolks, beaten
- ½ cup brown sugar
- 1/3 cup heavy cream
- 1 cup milk

1. Combine all the ingredients in a pan over medium heat.
2. Cook while stirring until temperature has reached 165 degrees F.
3. Let cool for 15 minutes.
4. Strain the mixture.
5. Transfer mixture to the Ninja Creami container.
6. Freeze for 24 hours.
7. Process using the Gelato function.

Strawberry Kiwi Sorbet

Prep time:5 minutes | Freeze Time:24 hours | Serves 4

- 2 cups strawberries, sliced
- 4 kiwi, sliced
- 1/8 cup raw agave
- 1/4 cup water

1. Add all the ingredients to your blender.
2. Blend until smooth.
3. Pour the mixture into the Ninja Creami pint container.
4. Freeze for 24 hours.
5. Transfer the container to the machine.
6. Select Sorbet function.

Red Velvet Gelato

Prep time:35 minutes | Freeze Time:24 hours | Serves 2

- 4 egg yolks
- 2 tablespoons cocoa powder
- ¼ cup granulated sugar
- 1 cup milk
- ¼ cup cream cheese
- 1/3 cup heavy cream
- 1 teaspoon red food coloring
- 1 teaspoon vanilla extract

1. Mix the egg yolks, cocoa powder and sugar in a bowl.
2. Stir in the rest of the ingredients.
3. Pour the mixture into a pan over medium heat.
4. Cook while stirring until the temperature has reached 165 degrees F.
5. Let cool for 20 minutes.
6. Transfer the mixture into the Ninja Creami pint container.
7. Freeze for 24 hours.
8. Add the container to the machine.
9. Select Gelato mode.

Strawberry And Champagne Delish Sorbet

Prep Time: 10 minutes | Cook time: 24 Hours 15 Minutes | Serves 2

- 2 ounces packet strawberry-flavored gelatin
- ¾ cup boiling water
- ½ cup light corn syrup
- 3 fluid ounces champagne
- 1 egg white, lightly beaten

1. Dissolve the gelatin in boiling water in a bowl. Beat in the corn syrup, champagne, and egg whites.
2. Put the mixture into the ninja CREAMi Pint container and freeze on a level surface in a cold freezer for a full 24 hours.
3. After 24 hours, remove the Pint from the freezer. Remove the lid.
4. Place the Ninja CREAMi Pint into the outer bowl. Place the outer bowl with the Pint into the ninja CREAMi machine and turn until the outer bowl locks into place. Push the SORBET button. During the SORBET function, the sorbet will mix together and become very creamy. This should take approximately 2 minutes.
5. Once the SORBET function has ended, turn the outer bowl and release it from the ninja CREAMi machine.
6. Your sorbet is ready to eat! Enjoy!

Blueberry & Crackers Gelato

Prep time: 10 minutes | Cook time: 3 minutes | Serves 4

- 4 large egg yolks
- 3 tablespoons granulated sugar
- 3 tablespoons wild blueberry preserves
- 1 teaspoon vanilla extract
- 1 cup whole milk
- ⅓ cup heavy cream
- ¼ cup cream cheese, softened
- 3-6 drops purple food coloring
- 2 large graham crackers, broken in 1-inch pieces

1. In a small saucepan, add the egg yolks, sugar, blueberry preserves and vanilla extract and beat until well combined.
2. Add the milk, heavy cream, cream cheese and food coloring and beat until well combined.
3. Place the saucepan over medium heat and cook for about 2-3 minutes, stirring continuously.
4. Remove from the heat and through a fine-mesh strainer, strain the mixture into an empty Ninja CREAMi pint container.
5. Place the container into an ice bath to cool.
6. After cooling, cover the container with the storage lid and freeze for 24 hours.
7. After 24 hours, remove the lid from container and arrange into the outer bowl of Ninja CREAMi. 8. Install the "Creamerizer Paddle" onto the lid of outer bowl.
8. Then rotate the lid clockwise to lock.
9. Press "Power" button to turn on the unit.
10. Then press "GELATO" button.
11. When the program is completed, with a spoon, create a 1½-inch wide hole in the center that reaches the bottom of the pint container.
12. Add the graham crackers into the hole and press "MIX-IN" button.
13. When the program is completed, turn the outer bowl and release it from the machine. 15. Transfer the gelato into serving bowls and serve immediately.

Coconut Lime Sorbet

Prep Time: 10 minutes | Cook time: 15 minutes| Serves 2

- 7 ounces can coconut cream
- ½ cup coconut water
- ¼ cup lime juice
- ½ tablespoon lime zest
- ¼ teaspoon coconut extract

1. Combine the coconut cream, coconut water, lime juice, lime zest, and coconut extract in a mixing bowl. Cover with plastic wrap and refrigerate for at least 1 hour, or until the flavors have melded.
2. Add the mixture to the Ninja CREAMi Pint container and freeze on a level surface in a cold freezer for a full 24 hours.
3. After 24 hours, remove the Pint from the freezer. Remove the lid.
4. Place the Ninja CREAMi Pint into the outer bowl. Place the outer bowl with the Pint into the ninja CREAMi machine and turn until the outer bowl locks into place. Push the SORBET button. During the SORBET function, the sorbet will mix together and become very creamy. This should take approximately 2 minutes.
5. Once the SORBET function has ended, turn the outer bowl and release it from the ninja CREAMi machine.
6. Your sorbet is ready to eat! Enjoy!

Cherry And Berry Sorbet

Prep Time: 10 minutes | Cook time: 24 Hours 10 Minutes| Serves 2

- 2 cups frozen cherry-berry fruit blend
- ¼ medium lemon, juiced
- ½ cup white sugar, to taste
- ½ cup rose wine

1. In a mixing bowl, combine all of the ingredients and stir until the sugar is completely dissolved. Place the mixture in the ninja CREAMi Pint container and freeze for a full 24 hours on a level surface in a cold freezer.
2. Remove the Pint from the freezer after 24 hours. Take off the lid.
3. In the outer bowl, place the Ninja CREAMi Pint. In the Ninja CREAMi machine, place the outer bowl with the Pint and turn until the outer bowl locks into place. Activate the SORBET function by pressing the SORBET button. The sorbet will mix together and become very creamy during the SORBET function. This should only take about 2 minutes.
4. Turn the outer bowl and remove it from the ninja CREAMi machine once the SORBET function has finished.
5. It's time to eat your sorbet! Enjoy!

Hearty Banana Sorbet

Prep Time: 10 minutes | Cook time: 24 Hours 10 Minutes| Serves 2

- 1 Frozen Banana
- 1 teaspoon cold water
- 2 teaspoons caramel sauce

1. Place the banana, water, and caramel sauce in the ninja CREAMi Pint container and freeze for a full 24 hours on a level surface in a cold freezer.
2. Remove the Pint from the freezer after 24 hours. Take off the lid.
3. In the outer bowl, place the Ninja CREAMi Pint. In the Ninja CREAMi machine, place the outer bowl with the Pint inside and turn until the outer bowl locks into place. Activate the SORBET function by pressing the SORBET button. The sorbet will mix together and become very creamy during the SORBET function. This should only take about 2 minutes.
4. Turn the outer bowl and remove it from the ninja CREAMi machine once the SORBET function has finished.
5. It's time to eat your sorbet! Enjoy!

Watermelon Lime Sorbet

Prep time: 5 minutes | Cook time: 24 hours 10 minutes| Serves 4

- 3½ cups seedless watermelon chunks
- 2 teaspoons lime juice
- ¼ cup warm water

1. Place all the ingredients in a blender. Mix well until smooth.
2. Pour the mixture into the Ninja CREAMi Pint and close the lid.
3. Place the pint into the freezer and freeze for 24 hours.
4. Once done, open the lid and place the pint into the outer bowl of the Ninja CREAMi. Set the Creamerizer Paddle into the outer bowl.
5. Lock the lid by rotating it clockwise.
6. Turn on the unit and press the SORBET button.
7. Once done, take out the bowl from the Ninja CREAMi.
8. Serve and enjoy your yummy sorbet.

Honey Blueberry Lemon Sorbet

Prep time: 5 minutes | Cook time: 10 minutes| Serves 4

- 3 cups fresh blueberries
- 2 tablespoons raw honey
- 3 tablespoons lemon juice
- 1 teaspoon lemon zest
- ⅓ cup water

1. Add the ingredients to a blender. Mix well until smooth.
2. Pour the mixture into the Ninja CREAMi Pint and close it with the lid.
3. Place the pint into the freezer and freeze for 24 hours.
4. Once done, open the lid and place the pint into the outer bowl of the Ninja CREAMi. Set the Creamerizer Paddle into the outer bowl.
5. Lock the lid by rotating it clockwise.
6. Turn the unit on and press the SORBET button.
7. Once done, take out the bowl from the Ninja CREAMi.
8. Serve and enjoy this yummy sorbet.

Cantaloupe Sorbet

Prep time: 5 minutes | Cook time: 10 minutes | Serves 4

- 3 cups cantaloupe pieces
- ⅓ cup water
- ⅓ cup organic sugar
- 1 tablespoon freshly squeezed lemon juice

1. Combine the cantaloupe, water, sugar, and lemon juice in a blender. Blend on high until smooth.
2. Pour the base into a clean CREAMi Pint. Place the storage lid on the container and freeze for 24 hours.
3. Remove the pint from the freezer and take off the lid. Place the pint in the outer bowl of your Ninja CREAMi, install the Creamerizer Paddle in the outer bowl lid, and lock the lid assembly onto the outer bowl. Place the bowl assembly on the motor base, and twist the handle to the right to raise the platform and lock it in place. Select the Sorbet function.
4. Once the machine has finished processing, remove the sorbet from the pint. Serve immediately.

Sweeet and Sour Mango Sorbet

Prep time: 5 minutes | Cook time: 15 minutes| Serves 4

- 4 cups mangoes, peeled, pitted and chopped
- ½ cup water
- ⅓-½ cup sugar
- ¼ cup fresh lime juice
- 2 tablespoons Chamoy

1. In a high-speed blender, add mangoes and water and pulse until smooth.
2. Through a fine-mesh strainer, strain the mango puree into a large bowl.
3. Add the sugar, lime juice and chamoy and stir to combine.
4. Transfer the mixture into an empty Ninja CREAMi pint container.
5. Cover the container with storage lid and freeze for 24 hours.
6. After 24 hours, remove the lid from container and arrange into the Outer Bowl of Ninja CREAMi.
7. Install the Creamerizer Paddle onto the lid of Outer Bowl.
8. Then rotate the lid clockwise to lock.
9. Press Power button to turn on the unit.
10. Then press Sorbet button.
11. When the program is completed, turn the Outer Bowl and release it from the machine.
12. Transfer the sorbet into serving bowls and serve immediately.

Rose Strawberry Sorbet

Prep time: 5 minutes | Cook time: 10 minutes| Serves 4

- 1¼ cups caster sugar
- 2 cups strawberries, hulled
- Juice of 1 lemon

1. Place all the ingredients in a blender. Mix well until smooth.
2. Pour the mixture into the Ninja CREAMi Pint and close it with the lid.
3. Place the pint into the freezer and freeze for 24 hours.
4. Once done, open the lid and place the pint into the outer bowl of the Ninja CREAMi. Set the Creamerizer Paddle into the outer bowl.
5. Lock the lid by rotating it clockwise.
6. Turn the unit on and press the SORBET button.
7. Once done, take out the bowl from the Ninja CREAMi.
8. Serve and enjoy the yummy sorbet.

Raspberry Strawberry Sorbet

Prep time: 5 minutes | Cook time: 10 minutes| Serves 2

- 2 strawberries, sliced
- 1 cup raspberries
- 2 cups water

1. Place the ingredients in a blender. Mix well until smooth.
2. Pour the mixture into the Ninja CREAMi Pint and close the lid.
3. Place the pint into the freezer and freeze for 24 hours.
4. Once done, open the lid and place the pint into the outer bowl of the Ninja CREAMi. Set the Creamerizer Paddle into the outer bowl.
5. Lock the lid by rotating it clockwise.
6. Turn the unit on and press the SORBET button.
7. Once done, take out the bowl from the Ninja CREAMi.
8. Serve and enjoy your yummy sorbet.

Orange Star Anise Sorbet

Prep time: 5 minutes | Cook time: 10 minutes| Serves 4

- 2 cups orange juice
- 2 teaspoons star anise
- ½ cup caster sugar

1. Add the ingredients to a blender. Mix well until smooth.
2. Pour the mixture into the Ninja CREAMi Pint and close the lid.
3. Place the pint into the freezer and freeze for 24 hours.
4. Once done, open the lid and place the pint into the outer bowl of the Ninja CREAMi. Set the Creamerizer Paddle into the outer bowl.
5. Lock the lid by rotating it clockwise.
6. Turn the unit on and press the SORBET button.
7. Once done, take out the bowl from the Ninja CREAMi.

Pomegranate & Blueberry Sorbet

Prep time: 5 minutes | Cook time: 10 minutes | Serves 4

- 1 (15-ounce) can blueberries in light syrup
- ½ cup pomegranate juice

1. In an empty Ninja CREAMi pint container, place the blueberries and top with syrup
2. Add in the pomegranate juice and stir to combine.
3. Cover the container with storage lid and freeze for 24 hours.
4. After 24 hours, remove the lid from container and arrange into the Outer bowl of Ninja CREAMi.
5. Install the Creamerizer Paddle onto the lid of Outer Bowl.
6. Then rotate the lid clockwise to lock.
7. Press Power button to turn on the unit.
8. Then press Sorbet button.
9. When the program is completed, turn the Outer Bowl and release it from the machine.
10. Transfer the sorbet into serving bowls and serve immediately.

Strawberries & Champagne Sorbet

Prep time: 5 minutes | Cook time: 24 hours 15 minutes | Serves 4

- 1 (2 ounces) packet strawberry-flavored gelatin (such as Jell-O)
- ¾ cup boiling water
- ½ cup light corn syrup
- 3 fluid ounces champagne
- 1 egg whites, slightly beaten

1. Dissolve the gelatin in boiling water in a bowl. Beat in the corn syrup, champagne, and egg whites.
2. Put the mixture into the ninja CREAMi Pint container and freeze on a level surface in a cold freezer for a full 24 hours.
3. After 24 hours, remove the Pint from the freezer. Remove the lid.
4. Place the Ninja CREAMi Pint into the outer bowl. Place the outer bowl with the Pint in it into the ninja CREAMi machine and turn until the outer bowl locks into place. Push the SORBET button. During the SORBET function, the sorbet will mix together and become very creamy. This should take approximately 2 minutes.
5. Once the SORBET function has ended, turn the outer bowl and release it from the ninja CREAMi machine.
6. Your sorbet is ready to eat! Enjoy!

Cherry Gelato

Prep time: 6 minutes | Cook time: 3 minutes | Serves 4

- 4 large egg yolks
- 1 tablespoon light corn syrup
- 5 tablespoons granulated sugar
- 1 cup heavy cream
- ⅓ cup whole milk
- 1 teaspoon almond extract
- 1 cup frozen black cherries, pitted and quartered

1. In a small saucepan, add the egg yolks, sugar and corn syrup and beat until well combined.
2. Add the heavy cream, milk and almond extract and beat until well combined.
3. Place the saucepan over medium heat and cook for about 2-3 minutes, stirring continuously.
4. Remove from the heat and through a fine-mesh strainer, strain the mixture into an empty Ninja CREAMi pint container.
5. Place the container into an ice bath to cool.
6. After cooling, cover the container with the storage lid and freeze for 24 hours.
7. After 24 hours, remove the lid from container and arrange into the outer bowl of Ninja CREAMi.
8. Install the "Creamerizer Paddle" onto the lid of outer bowl.
9. Then rotate the lid clockwise to lock.
10. Press "Power" button to turn on the unit.
11. Then press "GELATO" button.
12. When the program is completed, with a spoon, create a 1½-inch wide hole in the center that reaches the bottom of the pint container.
13. Add the cherries into the hole and press "MIX-IN" button.
14. When the program is completed, turn the outer bowl and release it from the machine. 15. Transfer the gelato into serving bowls and serve immediately.

Pecan Gelato

Prep time: 10 minutes | Cook time: 3 minutes | Serves 4

- 4 large egg yolks
- 5 tablespoons granulated sugar
- 1 tablespoon light corn syrup
- 1 cup heavy cream
- ⅓ cup whole milk
- 1 teaspoon butter flavor extract
- ⅓ cup pecans, chopped

1. In a small saucepan, add the egg yolks, sugar and corn syrup and beat until well combined.
2. Add the heavy cream, milk and butter flavor extract and beat until well combined.
3. Place the saucepan over medium heat and cook for about 2-3 minutes, stirring continuously.
4. Remove from the heat and through a fine-mesh strainer, strain the mixture into an empty Ninja CREAMi pint container.
5. Place the container into an ice bath to cool.
6. After cooling, cover the container with the storage lid and freeze for 24 hours.
7. After 24 hours, remove the lid from container and arrange into the outer bowl of Ninja CREAMi.
8. Install the "Creamerizer Paddle" onto the lid of outer bowl.
9. Then rotate the lid clockwise to lock.
10. Press "Power" button to turn on the unit.
11. Then press "GELATO" button.
12. When the program is completed, with a spoon, create a 1½-inch wide hole in the center that reaches the bottom of the pint container.
13. Add the pecans into the hole and press "MIX-IN" button.
14. When the program is completed, turn the outer bowl and release it from the machine. 15. Transfer the gelato into serving bowls and serve immediately.

Peanut Butter Gelato

Prep time: 20 minutes | Cook time: 10 minutes | Serves 4

- 1½ Cups unsweetened coconut milk
- 6 tablespoons sugar
- 1 tablespoon cornstarch
- 3 tablespoons peanut butter
- 3 dark chocolate peanut butter Cups, cut each into 8 pieces
- 2 tablespoons peanuts, chopped

1. In a small saucepan, add the coconut milk, sugar, and cornstarch and mix well.
2. Place the saucepan over medium heat and bring to a boil, beating continuously.
3. Reduce the heat to low and simmer for about 3-4 minutes.
4. Remove from the heat and stir in the peanut butter.
5. Transfer the mixture into an empty Ninja CREAMi pint container.
6. Place the container into an ice bath to cool.
7. After cooling, cover the container with the storage lid and freeze for 24 hours.
8. After 24 hours, remove the lid from container and arrange into the outer bowl of Ninja CREAMi.
9. Install the "Creamerizer Paddle" onto the lid of outer bowl.
10. Then rotate the lid clockwise to lock.
11. Press "Power" button to turn on the unit.
12. Then press "GELATO" button.
13. When the program is completed, with a spoon, create a 1½-inch wide hole in the center that reaches the bottom of the pint container.
14. Add the peanut butter Cup and peanuts into the hole and press "MIX-IN" button.
15. When the program is completed, turn the outer bowl and release it from the machine. 16. Transfer the gelato into serving bowls and serve immediately.

Marshmallow Gelato

Prep time: 20 minutes | Cook time: 5 minutes | Serves 4

- 1 cup whole milk
- ½ cup heavy cream
- ¼ cup sugar
- 3 egg yolk
- Pinch of sea salt
- ¼ cup mini marshmallows

1. Preheat the oven to broiler. Lightly grease a baking sheet.
2. Arrange the marshmallows onto the prepared baking sheet in a single layer.
3. Broil for about 5 minutes, flipping once halfway through.
4. Meanwhile, in a small saucepan, add the milk, heavy cream, sugar, egg yolks and a pinch of salt and beat until well combined.
5. Place the saucepan over medium heat and cook for about 1 minute, stirring continuously.
6. Remove from the heat and stir in half of the marshmallows.
7. Transfer the mixture into an empty Ninja CREAMi pint container.
8. Place the container into an ice bath to cool.
9. After cooling, cover the container with the storage lid and freeze for 24 hours.
10. Reserve the remaining marshmallows into the freezer.
11. After 24 hours, remove the lid from container and arrange into the outer bowl of Ninja CREAMi.
12. Install the "Creamerizer Paddle" onto the lid of outer bowl.
13. Then rotate the lid clockwise to lock.
14. Press "Power" button to turn on the unit.
15. Then press "GELATO" button.
16. When the program is completed, with a spoon, create a 1½-inch wide hole in the center that reaches the bottom of the pint container.
17. Add the reserved frozen marshmallows into the hole and press "MIX-IN" button.
18. When the program is completed, turn the outer bowl and release it from the machine. 19. Transfer the gelato into serving bowls and serve immediately.

Boozy Amaretto Cookie Milkshake

Prep time: 5 minutes | Freeze time: 24 hours| Serves 4

- 1 cup whole milk
- ½ cup amaretto-flavored coffee creamer
- ¼ cup amaretto liqueur
- 1 tablespoon agave nectar
- ¼ cup chopped chocolate chip cookies

1. In a clean CREAMi Pint, combine the milk, coffee creamer, amaretto liqueur, and agave. Stir well. Place the storage lid on the container and freeze for 24 hours.
2. Remove the pint from the freezer and take off the lid. Add the chocolate chip cookies to the top of the pint. Place the pint in the outer bowl of your Ninja® CREAMi™, install the Creamerizer™ Paddle in the outer bowl lid, and lock the lid assembly onto the outer bowl. Place the bowl assembly on the motor base, and twist the handle to the right to raise the platform and lock it in place. Select the Milkshake function.
3. Once the machine has finished processing, remove the lid. With a spoon, create a 1½-inch-wide hole that reaches the bottom of the pint. During this process, it is okay if your treat reaches above the Max Fill line. Add the chopped cookies to the hole in the pint, replace the lid, and select Milkshake. Serve immediately.

Chocolate Hazelnut Milkshake

Prep time: 5 minutes | Freeze time: 24 hours | Serves 4

- 2 tablespoons granulated sugar
- 2 tablespoons unsweetened cocoa powder
- ½ cup whole milk
- 1 cup hazelnut-flavored coffee creamer

1. In a large bowl, whisk together the sugar, cocoa powder, milk, and coffee creamer until the sugar is fully dissolved.
2. Pour the base into a clean CREAMi Pint. Place the storage lid on the container and freeze for 24 hours.
3. Remove the pint from the freezer and take off the lid. Place the pint in the outer bowl of your Ninja® CREAMi™, install the Creamerizer™ Paddle in the outer bowl lid, and lock the lid assembly onto the outer bowl. Place the bowl assembly on the motor base, and twist the handle to the right to raise the platform and lock it in place. Select the Milkshake function.
4. Once the machine has finished processing, remove the milkshake from the pint. Serve immediately.

Dairy-Free Strawberry Milkshake

Prep time: 2 minutes | Cook time: 5 minutes| Serves 4

- 1½ cups Coconut-Vanilla Ice Cream
- ½ cup oat milk
- 3 fresh strawberries

1. Combine the ice cream, oat milk, and strawberries in a clean CREAMi Pint.
2. Place the pint in the outer bowl of your Ninja® CREAMi™, install the Creamerizer™ Paddle in the outer bowl lid, and lock the lid assembly onto the outer bowl. Place the bowl assembly on the motor base, and twist the handle to the right to raise the platform and lock it in place. Select the Milkshake function.
3. Once the machine has finished processing, remove the milkshake from the pint. Serve immediately.

Chocolate-Peanut Butter Milkshake

Prep time: 2 minutes | Cook time: 5 minutes| Serves 2

- 1½ cups chocolate ice cream
- ½ cup whole milk
- ¼ cup mini peanut butter cups

1. Combine the chocolate ice cream and milk in a clean CREAMi Pint.
2. Use a spoon to create a 1½-inch-wide hole that goes all the way to the bottom of the pint. Pour the mini peanut butter cups into the hole.
3. Place the pint in the outer bowl of your Ninja® CREAMi™, install the Creamerizer™ Paddle in the outer bowl lid, and lock the lid assembly onto the outer bowl. Place the bowl assembly on the motor base, and twist the handle to the right to raise the platform and lock it in place. Select the Milkshake function.
4. Once the machine has finished processing, remove the milkshake from the pint. Serve immediately.

Avocado Milkshake

Prep time: 5 minutes | Cook time: 5 minutes | Serves 2

- 1 cup coconut ice cream
- 1 small ripe avocado, peeled, pitted and chopped
- 1 teaspoon fresh lemon juice
- 2 tablespoons agave nectar
- 1 teaspoon vanilla extract
- Pinch of salt
- ½ cup oat milk

1. In an empty Ninja CREAMi pint container, place ice cream, followed by remaining ingredients.
2. Arrange the container into the outer bowl of Ninja CREAMi.
3. Install the "Creamerizer Paddle" onto the lid of outer bowl.
4. Then rotate the lid clockwise to lock.
5. Press "Power" button to turn on the unit.
6. Then press "MILKSHAKE" button.
7. When the program is completed, turn the outer bowl and release it from the machine. 8. Transfer the shake into serving glasses and serve immediately.

Caramel Cone Milkshake

Prep time: 2 minutes | Cook time: 5 minutes| Serves 4

- 1½ cups vanilla ice cream
- ½ cup whole milk
- 3 tablespoons caramel sauce
- 1 waffle cone, crushed or finely chopped

1. Combine the vanilla ice cream, milk, and caramel sauce in a clean CREAMi Pint.
2. With a spoon, create a 1½-inch-wide hole that reaches the bottom of the pint. During this process, it is okay if your treat reaches above the Max Fill line. Add the crushed waffle cone to the hole in the pint.
3. Place the pint in the outer bowl of your Ninja® CREAMi™, install the Creamerizer™ Paddle in the outer bowl lid, and lock the lid assembly onto the outer bowl. Place the bowl assembly on the motor base, and twist the handle to the right to raise the platform and lock it in place. Select the Milkshake function.
4. Once the machine has finished processing, remove the milkshake from the pint. Serve immediately.

Cashew Butter Milkshake

Prep time: 10 minutes | Cook time: 5 minutes| Serves 2

- 1½ cups vanilla ice cream
- ½ cup canned cashew milk
- ¼ cup cashew butter

1. In an empty Ninja CREAMi pint container, place the ice cream.
2. Top with the remaining ingredients and gently stir to combine.
3. Arrange the container into the outer bowl of Ninja CREAMi.
4. Install the "Creamerizer Paddle" onto the lid of outer bowl.
5. Then rotate the lid clockwise to lock.
6. Press "Power" button to turn on the unit.
7. Then press "MILKSHAKE" button.
8. When the program is completed, turn the outer bowl and release it from the machine.
9. Transfer the shake into serving glasses and serve immediately.

Sugar Cookie Milkshake

Prep time: 10 minutes | Cook time: 5 minutes| Serves 1

- ½ cup vanilla ice cream
- ½ cup oat milk
- 1 small sugar cookie, crushed
- 2 tablespoons sprinkles

1. In an empty Ninja CREAMi pint container, place the ice cream.
2. With a spoon, create a 1½-inch wide hole in the center that reaches the bottom of the pint container.
3. Add the remaining ingredients into the hole.
4. Arrange the container into the outer bowl of Ninja CREAMi.
5. Install the "Creamerizer Paddle" onto the lid of outer bowl.
6. Then rotate the lid clockwise to lock.
7. Press "Power" button to turn on the unit.
8. Then press "MILKSHAKE" button.
9. When the program is completed, turn the outer bowl and release it from the machine.
10. Transfer the shake into a serving glass and serve immediately.

Chocolate Cherry Milkshake

Prep time: 10 minutes |Cook time: 5 minutes| Serves 2

- 1½ cups chocolate ice cream
- ½ cup canned cherries in syrup, drained
- ¼ cup whole milk

1. In an empty Ninja CREAMi pint container, place ice cream, followed by cherries and milk.
2. Arrange the container into the outer bowl of Ninja CREAMi.
3. Install the "Creamerizer Paddle" onto the lid of outer bowl.
4. Then rotate the lid clockwise to lock.
5. Press "Power" button to turn on the unit.
6. Then press "MILKSHAKE" button.
7. When the program is completed, turn the outer bowl and release it from the machine.
8. Transfer the shake into serving glasses and serve immediately.

Coconut Cashew Milkshake

Prep time: 5 minutes | Cook time: 24 hours 10 minutes| Serves 2

- 1½ cups vanilla coconut milk ice cream
- ½ cup canned full fat coconut milk
- ¼ cup cashew butter

1. Fill an empty CREAMi Pint with the ice cream.
2. Create a 1-inch wide hole in the bottom of the pint using a spoon. Fill the hole with the remaining ingredients.
3. Place the pint into the outer bowl of the Ninja CREAMi.
4. Install the Creamerizer Paddle onto the lid of the outer bowl, then rotate the lid clockwise to lock.
5. Turn on the unit.
6. Press the MILKSHAKE button.
7. When the program is complete, turn the outer bowl and release it from the machine.
8. Transfer the shake into serving glasses and serve immediately.

Banana Chocolate Milkshake

Prep time: 10 minutes|Cook time: 5 minutes| Serves 2

- 1½ cups chocolate ice cream
- ½ cup cashew milk
- ½ cup ripe banana, peeled and cut into ½-inch pieces
- 1 tablespoon instant coffee powder

1. In an empty Ninja CREAMi pint container, place ice cream, followed by milk, banana and coffee powder.
2. Arrange the container into the outer bowl of Ninja CREAMi.
3. Install the "Creamerizer Paddle" onto the lid of outer bowl.
4. Then rotate the lid clockwise to lock.
5. Press "Power" button to turn on the unit.
6. Then press "MILKSHAKE" button.
7. When the program is completed, turn the outer bowl and release it from the machine.
8. Transfer the shake into serving glasses and serve immediately.

Chocolate Cherry Milkshake

Prep time: 5 minutes | Cook time: 4 minutes | Serves 4

- 1½ cups chocolate ice cream
- ½ cup canned cherries in syrup, drained
- ¼ cup whole milk

1. In an empty Ninja CREAMi pint container, place ice cream followed by cherries and milk.
2. Arrange the container into the Outer Bowl of Ninja CREAMi.
3. Install the Creamerizer Paddle onto the lid of Outer Bowl.
4. Then rotate the lid clockwise to lock.
5. Press Power button to turn on the unit.
6. Then press Milkshake button.
7. When the program is completed, turn the Outer Bowl and release it from the machine. 8. Transfer the shake into serving glasses and serve immediately.

Coffee Vodka Milkshake

Prep time: 10 minutes|Cook time: 5 minutes| Serves 2

- 1 cup vanilla ice cream
- 2 tablespoons coffee liqueur
- 2 tablespoons vodka

1. In an empty Ninja CREAMi pint container, place ice cream, followed by coffee liqueur and vodka.
2. Arrange the container into the outer bowl of Ninja CREAMi.
3. Install the "Creamerizer Paddle" onto the lid of outer bowl.
4. Then rotate the lid clockwise to lock.
5. Press "Power" button to turn on the unit.
6. Then press "MILKSHAKE" button.
7. When the program is completed, turn the outer bowl and release it from the machine.
8. Transfer the shake into serving glasses and serve immediately.

Lemon Cookie Milkshake

Prep time: 5 minutes | Cook time: 10 minutes| Serves 4

- 1 cup vanilla ice cream
- 3 lemon cream sandwich cookies
- ¼ cup milk

1. Add the ice cream, lemon cream cookies, and milk into an empty CREAMi Pint.
2. Place the Pint in the outer bowl, install the Creamerizer Paddle onto the outer bowl lid and lock the lid assembly on the outer bowl. Place the bowl assembly on the motor base and crank the lever to elevate and secure the platform in place.
3. Select the MILKSHAKE option.
4. Remove the milkshake from the Pint after the processing is finished.

Chocolate Proyo Milkshake

Prep time: 5 minutes | Cook time: 24 hours 10 minutes | Serves 2

- 1 cup chocolate frozen yogurt
- 1 scoop chocolate protein whey powder
- 1 cup whole milk

1. Place all the ingredients in an empty Ninja CREAMi Pint and mix well.
2. Place the pint into the outer bowl of the Ninja CREAMi.
3. Install the Creamerizer Paddle onto the lid of the outer bowl, then rotate the lid clockwise to lock.
4. Turn the unit on.
5. Press the MILKSHAKE button.
6. When the program is complete, turn the outer bowl and release it from the machine.
7. Transfer the shake into serving glasses and serve immediately.

Vanilla Vodka Milkshake

Prep time: 10 minutes | Cook time: 5 minutes | Serves 2

- 2 cups French vanilla coffee creamer
- 1 tablespoon agave nectar
- 2 ounces (57 g) vodka
- 1 tablespoon rainbow sprinkles

1. In an empty Ninja CREAMi pint container, place all ingredients and mix well.
2. Cover the container with storage lid and freeze for 24 hours.
3. After 24 hours, remove the lid from container and arrange into the outer bowl of Ninja CREAMi.
4. Install the "Creamerizer Paddle" onto the lid of outer bowl.
5. Then rotate the lid clockwise to lock.
6. Press "Power" button to turn on the unit.
7. Then press "MILKSHAKE" button.
8. When the program is completed, turn the outer bowl and release it from the machine.
9. Transfer the shake into serving glasses and serve immediately.

Mocha Banana Milkshake

Prep time: 5 minutes | Cook time: 24 hours 5 minutes| Serves 2

1½ cups vegan chocolate ice cream
½ cup cashew milk
½ cup fresh ripe banana
1 tablespoon instant coffee powder

1. Fill an empty CREAMi Pint with the ice cream.
2. Create a 1½-inch wide hole in the bottom of the pint using a spoon. Fill the hole with the remaining ingredients.
3. Place the pint into the outer bowl of the Ninja CREAMi.
4. Install the Creamerizer Paddle onto the lid of the outer bowl, then rotate the lid clockwise to lock.
5. Turn on the unit.
6. Press the MILKSHAKE button.
7. When the program is complete, turn the outer bowl and release it from the machine.
8. Transfer the shake into serving glasses and serve immediately.

Peanut Butter Brownie Milkshake

Prep time: 5 minutes | Cook time: 10 minutes| Serves 4

- ½ cup chocolate ice cream
- ½ cup whole milk
- 2 tablespoons peanut butter, for mix-in
- 1¼ cups brownies, chopped into bite-sized pieces, for mix-in

1. Place the ice cream in an empty CREAMi Pint.
2. Use a spoon to create a 1½-inch wide hole that reaches the bottom of the Pint. Add the remaining ingredients to the hole.
3. Place Pint in outer bowl, install Creamerizer Paddle onto outer bowl lid and lock the lid assembly on the outer bowl. Place the bowl assembly on the motor base and crank the lever to elevate and secure the platform in place.
4. Select MILKSHAKE.
5. Remove the milkshake from the Pint after the processing is finished.

Cherry Chocolate Milkshake

Prep time: 5 minutes | Cook time: 10 minutes| Serves 4

- 1 cup chocolate ice cream
- ½ cup canned cherries in syrup, drained
- ¼ cup whole milk

1. Place all ingredients in an empty CREAMi Pint.
2. Place Pint in outer bowl, install Creamerizer Paddle onto outer bowl lid and lock the lid assembly on the outer bowl. Place the bowl assembly on the motor base and crank the lever to elevate and secure the platform in place.
3. Select MILKSHAKE.
4. Remove the milkshake from the Pint after the processing is finished.

Lemon Meringue Pie Milkshake

Prep time: 5 minutes | Cook time: 10 minutes| Serves 1

- 1 cup vanilla ice cream
- 4 tablespoons store-bought lemon curd, divided
- 4 tablespoons marshmallow topping, divided
- ½ cup Graham Crackers, broken, divided

1. Place the ice cream in an empty CREAMi Pint.
2. Use a spoon to create a 1½-inch wide hole that reaches the bottom of the Pint. Add the remaining ingredients to the hole.
3. Place Pint in outer bowl, install Creamerizer Paddle onto outer bowl lid and lock the lid assembly on the outer bowl. Place the bowl assembly on the motor base and crank the lever to elevate and secure the platform in place.
4. Select the MILKSHAKE option.
5. Remove the milkshake from the Pint after the processing is finished.

Peanut Butter and Jelly Milkshake

Prep time: 5 minutes | Cook time: 10 minutes| Serves 2

- 3 tablespoons peanut butter
- 3 tablespoons grape jelly
- 1 cup milk
- 5 ice cubes
- ½ teaspoon vanilla extract

1. Add the milk, peanut butter, ice cubes, vanilla extract, and grape jelly into an empty CREAMi Pint.
2. Place the Pint in the outer bowl, install the Creamerizer Paddle onto the outer bowl lid and lock the lid assembly on the outer bowl. Place the bowl assembly on the motor base and crank the lever to elevate and secure the platform in place.
3. Choose the MILKSHAKE option.
4. Remove the milkshake from the Pint after the processing is finished.

Healthy Strawberry Shake

Prep time: 5 minutes | Cook time: 10 minutes | Serves 1

- 1 cup milk
- 1 tablespoon honey
- ½ teaspoon vanilla extract
- ½ cup frozen strawberries

1. Add the milk, honey, vanilla extract, and strawberries into an empty CREAMi Pint.
2. Place Pint in outer bowl, install Creamerizer Paddle onto outer bowl lid and lock the lid assembly on the outer bowl. Place the bowl assembly on the motor base and crank the lever to elevate and secure the platform in place.
3. Select MILKSHAKE.
4. Remove the milkshake from the Pint after the processing is finished.

Chapter 6
Smoothie Recipes

Simple Smoothie Bowl

Prep time: 1 minute | Freeze time: 24 hours| Serves 4

- 1 (16-ounce) bottle fruit smoothie beverage

1. Pour the smoothie beverage into a clean CREAMi Pint. Place the storage lid on the container and freeze for 24 hours
2. Remove the pint from the freezer and take off the lid. Place the pint in the outer bowl of your Ninja® CREAMi™, install the Creamerizer™ Paddle in the outer bowl lid, and lock the lid assembly onto the outer bowl. Place the bowl assembly on the motor base, and twist the handle to the right to raise the platform and lock it in place. Select the Smoothie Bowl function.
3. Once the machine has finished processing, remove the smoothie bowl from the pint. Serve immediately with desired toppings.

Peaches and Cream Smoothie Bowl

Prep time: 5 minutes | Freeze time: 24 hours| Serves 4

- 1 (15-ounce) can peaches in their juice
- ¼ cup vanilla yogurt
- 2 tablespoons agave nectar

1. Place the peaches in their juice, yogurt, and agave in a clean CREAMi Pint and stir to combine. Place the storage lid on the container and freeze for 24 hours.
2. Remove the pint from the freezer and take off the lid. Place the pint in the outer bowl of your Ninja® CREAMi™, install the Creamerizer™ Paddle in the outer bowl lid, and lock the lid assembly onto the outer bowl. Place the bowl assembly on the motor base, and twist the handle to the right to raise the platform and lock it in place. Select the Smoothie Bowl function.
3. Once the machine has finished processing, remove the smoothie bowl from the pint. Serve immediately with desired toppings.

Chocolate Pumpkin Smoothie Bowl

Prep time: 5 minutes | Freeze time: 24 hours | Serves 4

- ½ cup canned pumpkin puree
- 2 tablespoons unsweetened cocoa powder
- 1 teaspoon pumpkin spice seasoning
- 2 ripe bananas, cut in ½-inch pieces
- 1 tablespoon agave nectar
- ¼ cup whole milk

1. In a small bowl, stir together the pumpkin puree, cocoa powder, and pumpkin spice until well combined. Pour the base into a clean CREAMi Pint. Mix in the bananas, agave, and milk until everything is fully combined and the bananas are coated. Place the storage lid on the container and freeze for 24 hours.
2. Remove the pint from the freezer and take off the lid. Place the pint in the outer bowl of your Ninja® CREAMi™, install the Creamerizer™ Paddle in the outer bowl lid, and lock the lid assembly onto the outer bowl. Place the bowl assembly on the motor base, and twist the handle to the right to raise the platform and lock it in place. Select the Smoothie Bowl function.
3. Once the machine has finished processing, remove the smoothie bowl from the pint. Serve immediately with your desired toppings.

Microwave Vanilla Cake

Prep time: 5 minutes | Cook Time: 2 minutes | Serves 4

- ½ teaspoon vanilla extract
- 3 tablespoons whole milk
- 2 tablespoons unsalted butter
- ⅛ teaspoon kosher salt
- ½ teaspoon baking powder
- 2 tablespoons granulated sugar
- ¼ cup all-purpose flour

1. Place all the ingredients except for the frosting in a clean CREAMi Pint container in the order listed.
2. Place the pint in the outer bowl of your Ninja® CREAMi™, install the Creamerizer™ Paddle in the outer bowl lid, and lock the lid assembly onto the outer bowl. Place the bowl assembly on the motor base, and twist the handle to the right to raise the platform and lock it in place. Select the Re-Spin function.
3. Once the machine has finished processing, place the pint container in the microwave and cook on High for 2 minutes (for a 1000-watt microwave). Check the cake for doneness—a skewer or knife inserted into the cake should come out clean, and the cake should pull away from the sides of the pint container.
4. Once the container is cool enough to handle, run a butter knife around the inside of the pint. Flip the pint over, and the cake should pop right out.
5. If you want to add frosting, slice the cake widthwise into 3 layers. Place one slice on a plate and frost the top of the layer. Lay a second slice on top of the first and frost the top. Top with the final slice of cake, then frost the top and sides of the assembled cake.
6. Cut in half and serve.

Banana Smoothie Bowl

Prep time: 10 minutes | Cook time: 1 minute | Serves 2

- ½ cup water
- ¼ cup quick oats
- 1 cup vanilla Greek yogurt
- ½ cup banana, peeled and sliced
- 3 tablespoons honey

1. In a small microwave-safe bowl, add the water and oats and microwave on High for about 1 minute
2. Remove from the microwave and stir in the yogurt, banana and honey until well combined.
3. Transfer the mixture into an empty Ninja CREAMi pint container.
4. Cover the container with storage lid and freeze for 24 hours.
5. After 24 hours, remove the lid from container and arrange into the outer bowl of Ninja CREAMi.
6. Install the "Creamerizer Paddle" onto the lid of outer bowl.
7. Then rotate the lid clockwise to lock.
8. Press "Power" button to turn on the unit.
9. Then press "SMOOTHIE BOWL" button.
10. When the program is completed, turn the outer bowl and release it from the machine.
11. Transfer the smoothie into serving bowls and serve with your favorite topping.

Raspberry Smoothie Bowl

Prep time: 10 minutes |Cook time: 5 minutes| Serves 2

- 2 cups fresh raspberries
- ½ cup vanilla yogurt
- ¼ cup fresh orange juice
- 1 tablespoon honey

1. In an empty Ninja CREAMi pint container, place the raspberries and with the back of a spoon, firmly press the berries below the MAX FILL line.
2. Add the yogurt, orange juice and honey and stir to combine.
3. Cover the container with the storage lid and freeze for 24 hours.
4. After 24 hours, remove the lid from container and arrange into the outer bowl of Ninja CREAMi.
5. Install the "Creamerizer Paddle" onto the lid of outer bowl.
6. Then rotate the lid clockwise to lock.
7. Press "Power" button to turn on the unit.
8. Then press "SMOOTHIE BOWL" button.
9. When the program is completed, turn the outer bowl and release it from the machine.
10. Transfer the smoothie into serving bowls and serve immediately.

Strawberry Smoothie Bowl

Prep time: 10 minutes|Cook time: 5 minutes| Serves 4

- 2 tablespoons vanilla protein powder
- ¼ cup agave nectar
- ¼ cup pineapple juice
- ½ cup whole milk
- 1 cup ripe banana, peeled and cut in ½-inch pieces
- 1 cup fresh strawberries, hulled and quartered

1. In a large bowl, add the protein powder, agave nectar, pineapple juice and milk and beat until well combined.
2. Place the banana and strawberry into an empty Ninja CREAMi pint container and with the back of a spoon, firmly press the fruit below the MAX FILL line.
3. Top with milk mixture and mix until well combined.
4. Cover the container with storage lid and freeze for 24 hours.
5. After 24 hours, remove the lid from container and arrange into the outer bowl of Ninja CREAMi.
6. Install the "Creamerizer Paddle" onto the lid of outer bowl.
7. Then rotate the lid clockwise to lock.
8. Press "Power" button to turn on the unit.
9. Then press "SMOOTHIE BOWL" button.
10. When the program is completed, turn the outer bowl and release it from the machine.
11. Transfer the smoothie into serving bowls and serve immediately.

Fruity Coffee Smoothie Bowl

Prep time: 10 minutes |Cook time: 5 minutes| Serves 4

- 1 cup brewed coffee
- ½ cup oat milk
- 1 tablespoons almond butter
- 1 cup fresh raspberries
- 1 large banana, peeled and sliced

1. In a high-speed blender add all the ingredients and pulse until smooth.
2. Transfer the mixture into an empty Ninja CREAMi pint container.
3. Cover the container with storage lid and freeze for 24 hours.
4. After 24 hours, remove the lid from container and arrange into the outer bowl of Ninja CREAMi.
5. Install the "Creamerizer Paddle" onto the lid of outer bowl.
6. Then rotate the lid clockwise to lock.
7. Press "Power" button to turn on the unit.
8. Then press "SMOOTHIE BOWL" button.
9. When the program is completed, turn the outer bowl and release it from the machine.
10. Transfer the smoothie into serving bowls and serve immediately.

Dragon Fruit Smoothie Bowl

Prep time: 10 minutes |Cook time: 5 minutes| Serves 4

- 2 cups frozen dragon fruit chunks
- 2 (6-ounce / 170-g) cans pineapple juice

1. Place the dragon fruit chunks into an empty Ninja CREAMi pint container.
2. Top with pineapple juice and stir to combine.
3. Cover the container with storage lid and freeze for 24 hours.
4. After 24 hours, remove the lid from container and arrange into the outer bowl of Ninja CREAMi.
5. Install the "Creamerizer Paddle" onto the lid of outer bowl.
6. Then rotate the lid clockwise to lock.
7. Press "Power" button to turn on the unit.
8. Then press "SMOOTHIE BOWL" button.
9. When the program is completed, turn the outer bowl and release it from the machine.
10. Transfer the smoothie into serving bowls and serve immediately.

Chocolate Fudge Frosting

Prep time: 5 minutes | Cook time: 5 minutes| Makes 1 pint

- ½ cup (1 stick) cold unsalted butter, cut in 8 pieces
- 1½ cups confectioners' sugar
- 2 tablespoons dark unsweetened cocoa powder
- 1 tablespoon heavy (whipping) cream
- 1 teaspoon vanilla extract

1. Place all the ingredients in a clean CREAMi Pint in the order listed.
2. Place the pint in the outer bowl of your Ninja® CREAMi™, install the Creamerizer™ Paddle in the outer bowl lid, and lock the lid assembly onto the outer bowl. Place the bowl assembly on the motor base, and twist the handle to the right to raise the platform and lock it in place. Select the Re-Spin function.
3. Once the machine has finished processing, the frosting should be smooth and easily scoopable with a spoon. If the frosting is too thick, select the Re-Spin function again and process until creamy and smooth.

Cranberry-Apple Pie Smoothie Bowl

Prep time: 5 minutes | Cook time: 10 minutes| Serves 4

- 1½ cups frozen cranberries
- ½ cup frozen cherries
- 1 cup apple juice
- ⅓ cup agave nectar
- ½ teaspoon ground cinnamon

1. Fill an empty CREAMi pint to the MAX FILL line with the frozen cranberries and cherries.
2. Whisk the agave nectar, apple juice, and cinnamon in a large mixing bowl until thoroughly blended.
3. Transfer the mixture into an empty Ninja CREAMi Pint.
4. Cover the pint with the lid and freeze for 24 hours.
5. After 24 hours, remove the lid and place the pint into the outer bowl of the Ninja CREAMi.
6. Install the Creamerizer Paddle onto the lid of the outer bowl, then rotate the lid clockwise to lock.
7. Turn the unit on.
8. Press the SMOOTHIE BOWL button.
9. When the program is complete, turn the outer bowl and release it from the machine.
10. Transfer the smoothie into serving bowls and serve with your favorite toppings.

Coconut Mango Smoothie Bowl

Prep time: 5 minutes | Cook time: 10 minutes| Serves 4

- 2 cups ripe mango, cubed
- 1 can unsweetened coconut milk

1. Mix all the ingredients until well combined in a large bowl.
2. Transfer the mixture into an empty Ninja CREAMi Pint.
3. Cover the pint with the lid and freeze for 24 hours.
4. After 24 hours, remove the lid and place the pint into the outer bowl of the Ninja CREAMi.
5. Install the Creamerizer Paddle onto the lid of the outer bowl, then rotate the lid clockwise to lock.
6. Turn the unit on.
7. Press the SMOOTHIE BOWL button.
8. When the program is complete, turn the outer bowl and release it from the machine.
9. Transfer the smoothie into serving bowls and serve with your favorite toppings.

Frozen Fruit Smoothie Bowl

Prep time: 5 minutes | Cook time: 3 minutes | Serves 2

- 1 ripe banana, peeled and cut in 1-inch pieces
- 2 cups frozen fruit mix
- 1¼ cups vanilla yogurt

1. In a large high-speed blender, add all the ingredients and pulse until smooth.
2. Transfer the mixture into an empty Ninja CREAMi pint container.
3. Cover the container with the storage lid and freeze for 24 hours.
4. After 24 hours, remove the lid from container and arrange into the outer bowl of Ninja CREAMi.
5. Install the "Creamerizer Paddle" onto the lid of outer bowl.
6. Then rotate the lid clockwise to lock.
7. Press "Power" button to turn on the unit.
8. Then press "SMOOTHIE BOWL" button.
9. When the program is completed, turn the outer bowl and release it from the machine. 10. Transfer the smoothie into serving bowls and serve immediately.

Mixed Berries Smoothie Bowl

Prep time: 5 minutes | Cook time: 10 minutes| Serves 4

- ¾ cup fresh strawberries, hulled and quartered
- ¾ cup fresh raspberries
- ¾ cup fresh blueberries
- ¾ cup fresh blackberries
- ¼ cup plain Greek yogurt
- 1 tablespoon honey

1. In an empty Ninja CREAMi pint container, place the berries and with the back of a spoon, firmly press the berries below the Max Fill line.
2. Add the yogurt and honey and stir to combine.
3. Cover the container with storage lid and freeze for 24 hours.
4. After 24 hours, remove the lid from container and arrange into the Outer Bowl of Ninja CREAMi.
5. Install the Creamerizer Paddle onto the lid of Outer Bowl.
6. Then rotate the lid clockwise to lock.
7. Press Power button to turn on the unit.
8. Then press Smoothie Bowl button.
9. When the program is completed, turn the Outer Bowl and release it from the machine.
10. Transfer the smoothie into serving bowls and serve immediately.

Peach and Grapefruit Smoothie Bowl

Prep time: 10 minutes|Cook time: 5 minutes| Serves 2

- 1 cup frozen peach pieces
- 1 cup vanilla Greek yogurt
- ¼ cup fresh grapefruit juice
- 2 tablespoons honey
- ¼ teaspoon vanilla extract
- ½ teaspoon ground cinnamon

1. In a high-speed blender, add all ingredients and pulse until smooth
2. Transfer the mixture into an empty Ninja CREAMi pint container.
3. Cover the container with the storage lid and freeze for 24 hours.
4. After 24 hours, remove the lid from container and arrange into the outer bowl of Ninja CREAMi.
5. Install the "Creamerizer Paddle" onto the lid of outer bowl.
6. Then rotate the lid clockwise to lock.
7. Press "Power" button to turn on the unit.
8. Then press "SMOOTHIE BOWL" button.
9. When the program is completed, turn the outer bowl and release it from the machine.
10. Transfer the smoothie into serving bowls and serve immediately.

Berries & Cherry Smoothie Bowl

Prep time: 5 minutes | Cook time: 10 minutes| Serves 4

- 1 cup cranberry juice cocktail
- ¼ cup agave nectar
- 2 cups frozen cherry berry blend

1. In a large bowl, add the agave nectar and cranberry juice cocktail and beat until well combined.
2. Place the cherry berry blend into an empty Ninja CREAMi pint container.
3. Top with cocktail mixture and stir to combine.
4. Cover the container with storage lid and freeze for 24 hours.
5. After 24 hours, remove the lid from container and arrange into the Outer Bowl of Ninja CREAMi.
6. Install the Creamerizer Paddle onto the lid of outer bowl.
7. Then rotate the lid clockwise to lock.
8. Press Power button to turn on the unit.
9. Then press Smoothie Bowl button.
10. When the program is completed, turn the Outer Bowl and release it from the machine.
11. Transfer the smoothie into serving bowls and serve immediately.

Mango & Raspberry Smoothie Bowl

Prep time: 5 minutes | Cook time: 10 minutes| Serves 2

- ¾ cup frozen mango chunks
- ½ cup frozen raspberries
- ½ cup whole milk Greek yogurt
- 2 tablespoons avocado flesh
- 1 tablespoon agave nectar

1. In a large bowl, add all the ingredients and mix well.
2. Transfer the mixture into an empty Ninja CREAMi pint container.
3. Cover the container with storage lid and freeze for 24 hours.
4. After 24 hours, remove the lid from container and arrange into the Outer Bowl of Ninja CREAMi.
5. Install the Creamerizer Paddle onto the lid of Outer Bowl.
6. Then rotate the lid clockwise to lock.
7. Press Power button to turn on the unit.
8. Then press Smoothie Bowl button.
9. When the program is completed, turn the Outer Bowl and release it from the machine.
10. Transfer the smoothie into serving bowls and serve immediately.

Mango & Orange Smoothie Bowl

Prep time: 5 minutes | Cook time: 10 minutes| Serves 2

- 1 cup frozen mango chunks
- 1 cup plain whole milk yogurt
- ¼ cup fresh orange juice
- 2 tablespoons maple syrup
- ½ teaspoon ground turmeric
- ⅛ teaspoon ground cinnamon
- ⅛ teaspoon ground ginger
- Pinch of ground black pepper

1. In a high-speed blender, add all ingredients and pulse until smooth
2. Transfer the mixture into an empty Ninja CREAMi pint container.
3. Cover the container with storage lid and freeze for 24 hours.
4. After 24 hours, remove the lid from container and arrange into the Outer Bowl of Ninja CREAMi.
5. Install the Creamerizer Paddle onto the lid of Outer Bowl.
6. Then rotate the lid clockwise to lock.
7. Press Power button to turn on the unit.
8. Then press Smoothie Bowl button.
9. When the program is completed, turn the Outer Bowl and release it from the machine.
10. Transfer the smoothie into serving bowls and serve immediately.

Chocolate, Peanut Butter & Banana Smoothie

Prep time: 5 minutes | Cook time: 5 minutes| Serves 2

- 1 (3¼ ounces) cup chocolate pudding
- 1 tablespoon creamy peanut butter
- 1 large ripe banana, cut into pieces
- ⅔ cup reduced-fat (2%) milk
- ½ cup ice cubes
- Reddi-wip chocolate dairy whipped topping

1. Mash the bananas in a large bowl and add all the other ingredients except for the whipped topping. Combine and put into the ninja CREAMi Pint.
2. Place the Pint into the outer bowl. Place the outer bowl with the Pint in it into the ninja CREAMi machine and turn until the outer bowl locks into place. Push the SMOOTHIE button. The ingredients will mix together and become very creamy.
3. Once the SMOOTHIE function has ended, turn the outer bowl and release it from the ninja CREAMi machine.
4. Scoop the smoothie into glass bowls to serve.

Gator Smoothies

Prep time: 5 minutes | Cook time: 5 minutes | Serves 1

- 1 cup ice
- 1 cup grape-flavored sports drink
- 1 scoop vanilla ice cream

1. Add the ice, sports drink, and ice cream into an empty ninja CREAMi Pint.
2. Place the Ninja CREAMi Pint into the outer bowl. Place the outer bowl with the Pint in it into the ninja CREAMi machine and turn until the outer bowl locks into place. Push the SMOOTHIE button. During the SMOOTHIE function, the ingredients will mix together and become very creamy.
3. Once the SMOOTHIE function has ended, turn the outer bowl and release it from the ninja CREAMi machine.
4. Pour into a tall glass.

Orange & Mango Smoothie Bowl

Prep time: 5 minutes | Cook time: 3 minutes | Serves 2

- 1 cup frozen mango chunks
- 1 cup plain whole milk yogurt
- ¼ cup fresh orange juice
- 2 tablespoons maple syrup
- ½ teaspoon ground turmeric
- ⅛ teaspoon ground cinnamon
- ⅛ teaspoon ground ginger
- Pinch of ground black pepper

1. In a high-speed blender, add all ingredients and pulse until smooth.
2. Transfer the mixture into an empty Ninja CREAMi pint container.
3. Cover the container with the storage lid and freeze for 24 hours.
4. After 24 hours, remove the lid from container and arrange into the outer bowl of Ninja CREAMi.
5. Install the "Creamerizer Paddle" onto the lid of outer bowl.
6. Then rotate the lid clockwise to lock.
7. Press "Power" button to turn on the unit.
8. Then press "SMOOTHIE BOWL" button.
9. When the program is completed, turn the outer bowl and release it from the machine. 10. Transfer the smoothie into serving bowls and serve immediately.

Energy Elixir Smoothie

Prep time: 5 minutes | Cook time: 5 minutes | Serves 1

- ½ cup spring salad greens
- ½ cup frozen red grapes
- ½ chopped frozen banana
- ½ cored and chopped frozen pear
- 2 tablespoons walnuts
- Water as needed

1. Layer the salad greens, red grapes, banana, pear, walnuts, and enough water to cover the mixture in an empty ninja CREAMi Pint.
2. Place the Ninja CREAMi Pint into the outer bowl. Place the outer bowl with the Pint in it into the ninja CREAMi machine and turn until the outer bowl locks into place. Push the SMOOTHIE button. During the SMOOTHIE function, the ingredients will mix together and become very creamy.
3. Once the SMOOTHIE function has ended, turn the outer bowl and release it from the ninja CREAMi machine.
4. Scoop the smoothie into a glass.

Chapter 7
Ice Cream Mix Ins

Vanilla Pecan Ice Cream

Prep time: 5 minutes | Cook time: 10 minutes| Serves 6

- 1 cup whole milk
- ¾ cup heavy cream
- ⅓ cup granulated sugar
- ½ cup toasted pecans, coarsely chopped
- 5 pecan shortbread cookies
- ½ cup potato chips, crushed

1. Place all the ingredients in a blender. Mix well until smooth.
2. Pour the mixture into the Ninja CREAMi Pint and close it with the lid.
3. Place the pint into the freezer and freeze for 24 hours.
4. Once done, remove the lid and place the pint into the outer bowl of the Ninja CREAMi. Secure the Creamerizer Paddle into the outer bowl.
5. Lock the lid by rotating it clockwise.
6. Turn on the unit and press the ICE CREAM button.
7. Once done, take out the bowl from the Ninja CREAMi.

Vanilla Blueberry Ice Cream

Prep time: 5 minutes | Cook time: 10 minutes| Serves 6

- 6 pie crusts
- 1 cup whole milk
- ¾ cup heavy cream
- ⅓ cup granulated sugar
- 1 large egg, beaten
- ½ cup frozen blueberries, thawed

1. Place the ingredients in a blender. Mix well until smooth.
2. Pour the mixture into the Ninja CREAMi Pint and close it with the lid.
3. Place the pint into the freezer for 24 hours.
4. Once frozen, remove the lid and set the pint into the outer bowl of the Ninja CREAMi. Set the Creamerizer Paddle into the outer bowl.
5. Lock the lid by rotating it clockwise.
6. Turn the unit on and then press the ICE CREAM button.
7. Once done, take out the bowl from the Ninja CREAMi.
8. Serve and enjoy.

Orange Chunk Chocolate Ice Cream

Prep time: 5 minutes | Cook time: 10 minutes| Serves 2

- 2 tablespoons orange zest, grated
- 1 cup white chocolate, chopped
- 1 cup whole milk
- ¾ cup heavy cream
- 2 tablespoons mini chocolate chips
- 2 tablespoons cocoa powder
- ⅓ cup granulated sugar

1. Place all the ingredients in a blender. Mix well until smooth.
2. Pour the mixture into the Ninja CREAMi Pint and close the lid.
3. Place the pint into the freezer and freeze for 24 hours.
4. Once done, open the lid and place the pint into the outer bowl of the Ninja CREAMi. Set the Creamerizer Paddle into the outer bowl.
5. Lock the lid by rotating it clockwise.
6. Turn the unit on and press the ICE CREAM button.
7. Once done, take out the bowl from the Ninja CREAMi.
8. Serve and enjoy your delicious ice cream.

Lavender Cookie Ice Cream

Prep time: 5 minutes | Cook time: 10 minutes| Serves 4

- ¾ cup heavy cream
- 1 tablespoon dried culinary lavender
- ⅛ teaspoon salt
- ¾ cup whole milk
- ½ cup sweetened condensed milk
- 4 drops purple food coloring
- ⅓ cup chocolate wafer cookies, crushed

1. In a medium saucepan, add heavy cream, lavender and salt and mix well.
2. Place the saucepan over low heat and steep, covered for about ten minutes, stirring after every two minutes.
3. Remove from the heat and through a fine-mesh strainer, strain the cream mixture into a large bowl.
4. Discard the lavender leaves.
5. In the bowl of cream mixture, add the milk, condensed milk and purple food coloring and beat until smooth.
6. Transfer the mixture into an empty Ninja CREAMi pint container.
7. Cover the container with storage lid and freeze for 24 hours.
8. After 24 hours, remove the lid from container and arrange into the Outer Bowl of Ninja CREAMi.
9. Install the Creamerizer Paddle onto the lid of Outer Bowl.
10. Then rotate the lid clockwise to lock.
11. Press Power button to turn on the unit.
12. Then press Ice Cream button.
13. When the program is completed, with a spoon, create a 1½-inch wide hole in the center that reaches the bottom of the pint container.
14. Add the crushed cookies the hole and press Mix-In button.
15. When the program is completed, turn the Outer Bowl and release it from the machine.
16. Transfer the ice cream into serving bowls and serve immediately.

Mint Cookies Ice Cream

Prep time: 5 minutes | Cook time: 15 minutes | Serves 4

- ¾ cup coconut cream
- ¼ cup monk fruit sweetener with Erythritol
- 2 tablespoons agave nectar
- ½ teaspoon mint extract
- 5-6 drops green food coloring
- 1 cup oat milk
- 3 chocolate sandwich cookies, quartered

1. 1n a large bowl, add the coconut cream and beat until smooth.
2. Add the sweetener, agave nectar, mint extract and food coloring and beat until sweetener is dissolved.
3. Add the oat milk and beat until well combined.
4. Transfer the mixture into an empty Ninja CREAMi pint container.
5. Cover the container with storage lid and freeze for 24 hours.
6. After 24 hours, remove the lid from container and arrange into the Outer Bowl of Ninja CREAMi.
7. Install the Creamerizer Paddle onto the lid of Outer Bowl.
8. Then rotate the lid clockwise to lock.
9. Press Power button to turn on the unit.
10. Then press Lite Ice Cream button.
11. When the program is completed, with a spoon, create a 1½-inch wide hole in the center that reaches the bottom of the pint container.
12. Add the cookie pieces into the hole and press Mix-In button.
13. When the program is completed, turn the Outer Bowl and release it from the machine.
14. Transfer the ice cream into serving bowls and serve immediately.

Vanilla Ice Cream With Chocolate Chips

Prep time: 5 minutes | Cook time: 24 hours 10 minutes | Serves 4

- 1 tablespoon cream cheese, softened
- ⅓ cup granulated sugar
- 1 teaspoon vanilla extract
- ¾ cup heavy cream
- 1 cup whole milk
- ¼ cup mini chocolate chips, for mix-in

1. Microwave the cream cheese for 10 seconds in a large microwave-safe bowl. With a rubber spatula, blend in the sugar and vanilla extract until the mixture resembles frosting, about 60 seconds.
2. Slowly whisk in the heavy cream and milk until smooth and the sugar has dissolved.
3. Pour the base into an empty CREAMi Pint. Place the storage lid on the Pint and freeze for 24 hours.
4. Remove the Pint from the freezer and remove the lid from the Pint. Place the Pint in the outer bowl, install the Creamerizer Paddle onto the outer bowl lid, and lock the lid assembly on the outer bowl. Select ICE CREAM.
5. With a spoon, create a 1½-inch wide hole that reaches the bottom of the Pint. During this process, it's okay for your treat to press above the max fill line. Add chocolate chips to the hole in the Pint and process again using the MIX-IN program.
6. When processing is complete, remove the ice cream from the Pint.

Mint Chocolate Chip Ice Cream

Prep time: 5 minutes | Cook time: 24 hours 10 minutes | Serves 4

- 1 tablespoon cream cheese, softened
- ⅓ cup granulated sugar
- 1 teaspoon vanilla extract
- ¾ cup heavy cream
- 1 cup whole milk
- 1 teaspoon mint extract
- Green food coloring (optional)
- ¼ cup mini chocolate chips, for mix-in

1. Microwave the cream cheese for 10 seconds in a large microwave-safe bowl. Combine with the sugar and mint extract in a mixing bowl using a whisk or rubber spatula for about 60 seconds or until the mixture resembles frosting.
2. Slowly whisk in the heavy cream, milk, and optional food coloring until thoroughly mixed and the sugar has dissolved.
3. Pour the base into an empty CREAMi Pint. Place the storage lid on the Pint and freeze for 24 hours.
4. Remove the Pint from the freezer and remove its lid. Place the Pint in the outer bowl, install the Creamerizer Paddle onto the outer bowl lid, and lock the lid assembly on the outer bowl. Place the bowl assembly on the motor base, twist the handle to raise the platform, and lock it in place.
5. Select ICE CREAM.
6. With a spoon, create a 1½-inch wide hole that reaches the bottom of the Pint. During this process, it's okay for your treat to press above the max fill line. Add the chocolate chips to the hole and process again using the MIX-IN program.
7. When processing is complete, remove the ice cream from the Pint.

Jelly & Peanut Butter Ice Cream

Prep time: 5 minutes | Cook time:5 minutes | Serves 4

- 3 tablespoons granulated sugar
- 4 large egg yolks
- 1 cup whole milk
- ⅓ cup heavy cream
- ¼ cup smooth peanut butter
- 3 tablespoons grape jelly
- ¼ cup honey roasted peanuts, chopped

1. 1n a small saucepan, add the sugar and egg yolks and beat until sugar is dissolved.
2. Add the milk, heavy cream, peanut butter, and grape jelly to the saucepan and stir to combine.
3. Place saucepan over medium heat and cook until temperature reaches cook until temperature reaches to 165 -175° F, stirring continuously with a rubber spatula.
4. Remove from the heat and through a fine-mesh strainer, strain the mixture into an empty Ninja CREAMi pint container.
5. Place the container into ice bath to cool.
6. After cooling, cover the container with storage lid and freeze for 24 hours.
7. After 24 hours, remove the lid from container and arrange into the Outer Bowl of Ninja CREAMi.
8. Install the Creamerizer Paddle onto the lid of Outer Bowl.
9. Then rotate the lid clockwise to lock.
10. Press Power button to turn on the unit.
11. Then press ICE CREAM button.
12. When the program is completed, with a spoon, create a 1½-inch wide hole in the center that reaches the bottom of the pint container.
13. Add the peanuts into the hole and press Mix-In button.
14. When the program is completed, turn the Outer Bowl and release it from the machine.
15. Transfer the ice cream into serving bowls and serve immediately.

Chocolate Brownie Ice Cream

Prep time: 5 minutes | Cook time: 15 minutes| Serves 4

- 1 tablespoon cream cheese, softened
- ⅓ cup granulated sugar
- 1 teaspoon vanilla extract
- 2 tablespoons cocoa powder
- 1 cup whole milk
- ¾ cup heavy cream
- 2 tablespoons mini chocolate chips
- 2 tablespoons brownie chunks

1. 1n a large microwave-safe bowl, add the cream cheese and microwave on High for about ten seconds.
2. Remove from the microwave and stir until smooth.
3. Add the sugar and almond extract and with a wire whisk, beat until the mixture looks like frosting.
4. Slowly add the milk and heavy cream and beat until well combined.
5. Transfer the mixture into an empty Ninja CREAMi pint container.
6. Cover the container with storage lid and freeze for 24 hours.
7. After 24 hours, remove the lid from container and arrange into the Outer Bowl of Ninja CREAMi.
8. Install the Creamerizer Paddle onto the lid of Outer Bowl.
9. Then rotate the lid clockwise to lock.
10. Press Power button to turn on the unit.
11. Then press Ice Cream button.
12. When the program is completed, with a spoon, create a 1½-inch wide hole in the center that reaches the bottom of the pint container.
13. Add the chocolate chunks and brownie pieces into the hole and press Mix-In button.
14. When the program is completed, turn the Outer Bowl and release it from the machine.
15. Transfer the ice cream into serving bowls and serve immediately.

Cookies And Coconut Ice Cream

Prep time: 5 minutes | Cook time: 3 minutes | Serves 4

- 1 can full-fat unsweetened coconut milk
- ½ cup organic sugar
- 1 teaspoon vanilla extract
- 4 chocolate sandwich cookies, crushed

1. In a medium bowl, whisk together the coconut milk, sugar, and vanilla until well combined and the sugar is dissolved.
2. Pour the base into a clean CREAMi Pint. Place the storage lid on the container and freeze for 24 hours.
3. Remove the pint from the freezer and take off the lid. Place the pint in the outer bowl of your Ninja CREAMi, install the Creamerizer Paddle in the outer bowl lid, and lock the lid assembly onto the outer bowl. Place the bowl assembly on the motor base, and twist the handle to the right to raise the platform and lock it in place. Select the Ice Cream function.
4. Once the machine has finished processing, remove the lid from the pint container. With a spoon, create a 1½-inch-wide hole that reaches the bottom of the pint. During this process, it is okay if your treat reaches above the Max Fill line. Add the crushed cookies to the hole in the pint, replace the lid, and select the Mix-In function.
5. Once the machine has finished processing, remove the ice cream from the pint. Serve immediately with desired toppings.

Cinnamon Sugar Cookie Ice Cream

Prep time: 5 minutes | Cook time: 10 minutes| Serves 4

- 3 to 6 sugar cookies
- ½ teaspoon ground cinnamon
- 1 cup whole milk
- ¾ cup heavy cream
- ⅓ cup granulated sugar

1. Take a blender and add the ingredients to it. Mix well until smooth.
2. Pour the mixture into the Ninja CREAMi Pint and close the lid.
3. Place the pint into the freezer and freeze for 24 hours.
4. Once done, open the lid and place the pint into the outer bowl of the Ninja CREAMi. Set the Creamerizer Paddle into the outer bowl.
5. Lock the lid by rotating it clockwise.
6. Turn on the unit and then press the ICE CREAM button.
7. Once done, take out the bowl from the Ninja CREAMi.
8. Serve and enjoy.

Lavender Cookies & Cream Ice Cream

Prep time: 5 minutes | Cook time: 24 hours 10 minutes| Serves 4

- ½ cup heavy cream
- ½ tablespoon dried culinary lavender
- ¼ teaspoon kosher salt
- ½ cup whole milk
- ¼ cup sweetened condensed milk
- 2 drops purple food coloring
- ¼ cup crushed chocolate wafer cookies

1. Whisk together the heavy cream, lavender, and salt in a medium saucepan.
2. Steep the mixture for 10 minutes over low heat, stirring every 2 minutes to prevent bubbling.
3. Using a fine-mesh strainer, drain the lavender from the heavy cream into a large mixing basin. Discard the lavender.
4. Combine the milk, sweetened condensed milk, and purple food coloring in a large mixing bowl. Whisk until the mixture is completely smooth.
5. Pour the base into an empty CREAMi Pint. Place the Pint into an ice bath. Once cooled, place the storage lid on the Pint and freeze for 24 hours.
6. Remove the Pint from the freezer and remove its lid. Place Pint in outer bowl, install Creamerizer Paddle in outer bowl lid, and lock the lid assembly onto the outer bowl. Select ICE CREAM.
7. When the process is done, create a 1½-inch wide hole that reaches the bottom of the Pint with a spoon. It's okay if your treat exceeds the max fill line. Add crushed wafer cookies to the hole and process again using the MIX-IN program.
8. When processing is complete, remove ice cream from Pint and serve immediately, topped with extra crumbled wafers if desired.

Vanilla Peanut Butter Ice Cream

Prep time: 5 minutes | Cook time: 10 minutes| Serves 4

- ½ cup peanut butter cups, chopped
- ¼ cup peanut butter chips
- ½ cup salted pretzels, crushed
- 1 cup whole milk
- ¾ cup heavy cream
- ⅓ cup granulated sugar

1. Add the ingredients to a blender. Mix well until smooth.
2. Pour the mixture into the Ninja CREAMi Pint and close it with the lid.
3. Place the pint into the freezer and freeze for 24 hours.
4. Once done, open the lid and set the pint into the outer bowl of the Ninja CREAMi. Put the Creamerizer Paddle into the outer bowl.
5. Lock the lid by rotating it clockwise.
6. Turn on the unit and press the ICE CREAM button.
7. Once done, take out the bowl from the Ninja CREAMi.
8. Serve and enjoy.

Lite Chocolate Cookie Ice Cream

Prep time: 5 minutes | Cook time: 24 hours 10 minutes| Serves 2

- 1 tablespoon cream cheese, at room temperature
- 2 tablespoons unsweetened cocoa powder
- ½ teaspoon stevia sweetener
- 3 tablespoons raw agave nectar
- 1 teaspoon vanilla extract
- ¾ cup heavy cream
- 1 cup whole milk
- ¼ cup crushed reduced-fat sugar cookies

1. Place the cream cheese in a large microwave-safe bowl and heat on high for 10 seconds.
2. Mix in the cocoa powder, stevia, agave, and vanilla. Microwave for 60 seconds more, or until the mixture resembles frosting.
3. Slowly whisk in the heavy cream and milk until the sugar has dissolved and the mixture is thoroughly mixed.
4. Pour the base into a clean CREAMi Pint. Place the storage lid on the container and freeze for 24 hours.
5. Remove the Pint from the freezer and take off the lid. Place the Pint in the outer bowl of your Ninja CREAMi, install the Creamerizer Paddle in the outer bowl lid, and lock the lid assembly onto the outer bowl. Place the bowl assembly on the motor base, and twist the handle to the right to raise the platform and lock it in place. Select the LITE ICE CREAM function.
6. Once the machine has finished processing, remove the lid. With a spoon, create a 1½-inch-wide hole that reaches the bottom of the Pint. During this process, it's okay if your treat goes above the max fill line. Add the crushed cookies to the hole in the Pint. Replace the Pint lid and select the MIX-IN function.
7. Once the machine has finished processing, remove the ice cream from the Pint.

Rocky Road Ice Cream

Prep time: 5 minutes | Cook time: 3 minutes | Serves 4

- 1 cup whole milk
- ½ cup frozen cauliflower florets, thawed
- ½ cup dark brown sugar
- 3 tablespoons dark cocoa powder
- 1 teaspoon chocolate extract
- ⅓ cup heavy cream
- 2 tablespoons almonds, sliced
- 2 tablespoons mini marshmallows
- 2 tablespoons mini chocolate chips

1. In a high-speed blender, add milk, cauliflower, brown sugar, cocoa powder, and chocolate extract and pulse until smooth.
2. Transfer the mixture into an empty Ninja CREAMi pint container.
3. Add the heavy cream and stir until well combined.
4. Cover the container with storage lid and freeze for 24 hours.
5. After 24 hours, remove the lid from container and arrange into the Outer Bowl of Ninja CREAMi.
6. Install the Creamerizer Paddle onto the lid of Outer Bowl.
7. Then rotate the lid clockwise to lock. 8. Press Power button to turn on the unit.
8. Then press Ice Cream button.
9. When the program is completed, with a spoon, create a 1½-inch wide hole in the center that reaches the bottom of the pint container.
10. Add the almonds, marshmallows and chocolate chips into the hole and press Mix-In button.
11. When the program is completed, turn the Outer Bowl and release it from the machine.
12. Transfer the ice cream into serving bowls and serve immediately.

Sneaky Mint Chip Ice Cream

Prep time: 5 minutes | Cook time: 3 minutes | Serves 4

- 3 large egg yolks
- 1 tablespoon corn syrup
- ¼ cup granulated sugar
- ⅓ cup whole milk
- ¾ cup heavy (whipping) cream
- 1 cup packed fresh spinach
- ½ cup frozen peas, thawed
- 1 teaspoon mint extract
- ¼ cup semisweet chocolate chips

1. Fill a large bowl with ice water and set it aside.
2. In a small saucepan, whisk together the egg yolks, corn syrup, and sugar until the mixture is fully combined and the sugar is dissolved. Do not do this over heat.
3. Whisk in the milk and heavy cream.
4. Place the pan over medium heat. Cook, stirring constantly with a rubber spatula, until the temperature reaches 165°F to 175°F on an instant-read thermometer.
5. Remove the pan from the heat and pour the base into a clean CREAMi Pint. Carefully place the container in the prepared ice water bath, making sure the water doesn't spill into the base.
6. Once the mixture has completely cooled, pour the base into a blender and add the spinach, peas, and mint extract. Blend on high for 30 seconds. Strain the base through a fine-mesh strainer back into the CREAMi Pint. Place the storage lid on the container and freeze for 24 hours.
7. Remove the pint from the freezer and take off the lid. Place the pint in the outer bowl of your Ninja CREAMi, install the Creamerizer Paddle in the outer bowl lid, and lock the lid assembly onto the outer bowl. Place the bowl assembly on the motor base, and twist the handle to the right to raise the platform and lock it in place. Select the Ice Cream function.
8. Once the machine has finished processing, remove the lid from the pint container. With a spoon, create a 1½-inch-wide hole that reaches the bottom of the pint. During this process, it is okay if your treat reaches above the Max Fill line. Add the chocolate chips to the hole in the pint, replace the lid, and select the Mix-In function.
9. Once the machine has finished processing, remove the ice cream from the pint. Serve immediately.

Bourbon-maple walnut Ice Cream

Prep time: 5 minutes | Cook time: 3 minutes | Serves 4

- 4 large egg yolks
- ¼ cup maple syrup
- ¼ cup corn syrup
- 2 tablespoons bourbon
- ½ cup whole milk
- 1 cup heavy (whipping) cream
- ¼ cup toasted walnut halves

1. Fill a large bowl with ice water and set it aside.
2. In a small saucepan, whisk together the egg yolks, maple syrup, corn syrup, and bourbon until the mixture is fully combined. Do not do this over heat.
3. Whisk in the milk and heavy cream.
4. Place the pan over medium heat. Cook, stirring constantly with a rubber spatula, until the temperature reaches 165°F to 175°F on an instant-read thermometer.
5. Remove the pan from the heat and pour the base into a clean CREAMi Pint. Carefully place the container in the prepared ice water bath, making sure the water doesn't spill into the base.
6. Once the base has cooled, place the storage lid on the pint and freeze for 24 hours.
7. Remove the pint from the freezer and take off the lid. Place the pint in the outer bowl of your Ninja CREAMi, install the Creamerizer Paddle in the outer bowl lid, and lock the lid assembly onto the outer bowl. Place the bowl assembly on the motor base, and twist the handle to the right to raise the platform and lock it in place. Select the Ice Cream function.
8. Once the machine has finished processing, remove the lid from the pint container. With a spoon, create a 1½-inch-wide hole that reaches the bottom of the pint. During this process, it is okay if your treat reaches above the Max Fill line. Add the toasted walnuts to the hole in the pint, replace the lid, and select the Mix-In function.
9. Once the machine has finished processing, remove the ice cream from the pint. Serve immediately.

Fruity Cereal Ice Cream

Prep time: 5 minutes | Cook time: 30 minutes | Serves 2

- ¾ cup whole milk
- 1 cup fruity cereal, divided
- 1 tablespoon Philadelphia cream cheese, softened
- ¼ cup granulated sugar
- 1 teaspoon vanilla extract
- ½ cup heavy cream

1. In a large mixing bowl, combine ½ cup of the fruity cereal and the milk. Allow the mixture to settle for 15–30 minutes, stirring occasionally to infuse the milk with the fruity taste.
2. Microwave the Philadelphia cream cheese for 10 seconds in a second large microwave-safe dish. Combine the sugar and vanilla extract in a mixing bowl with a whisk or rubber spatula until the mixture resembles frosting, about 60 seconds.
3. After 15 to 30 minutes, sift the milk and cereal into the bowl with the sugar mixture using a fine-mesh filter. To release extra milk, press on the cereal with a spoon, then discard it. Mix in the heavy cream until everything is thoroughly mixed.
4. Pour the mixture into an empty ninja CREAMi Pint container. Add the strawberries to the Pint, making sure not to go over the max fill line, and freeze for 24 hours.
5. After 24 hours, remove the Pint from the freezer. Remove the lid.
6. Place the Ninja CREAMi Pint into the outer bowl. Place the outer bowl with the Pint in it into the ninja CREAMi machine and turn until the outer bowl locks into place. Push the ICE CREAM button. During the ICE CREAM function, the ice cream will mix together and become very creamy.
7. Use a spoon to create a 1½-inch wide hole that reaches the bottom of the Pint. Add the remaining ½ cup of fruity cereal to the hole and process again using the mix-in. When processing is complete, remove the ice cream from the Pint.

Appendix 1 Measurement Conversion Chart

Volume Equivalents (Dry)

US STANDARD	METRIC (APPROXIMATE)
1/8 teaspoon	0.5 mL
1/4 teaspoon	1 mL
1/2 teaspoon	2 mL
3/4 teaspoon	4 mL
1 teaspoon	5 mL
1 tablespoon	15 mL
1/4 cup	59 mL
1/2 cup	118 mL
3/4 cup	177 mL
1 cup	235 mL
2 cups	475 mL
3 cups	700 mL
4 cups	1 L

Weight Equivalents

US STANDARD	METRIC (APPROXIMATE)
1 ounce	28 g
2 ounces	57 g
5 ounces	142 g
10 ounces	284 g
15 ounces	425 g
16 ounces (1 pound)	455 g
1.5 pounds	680 g
2 pounds	907 g

Volume Equivalents (Liquid)

US STANDARD	US STANDARD (OUNCES)	METRIC (APPROXIMATE)
2 tablespoons	1 fl.oz.	30 mL
1/4 cup	2 fl.oz.	60 mL
1/2 cup	4 fl.oz.	120 mL
1 cup	8 fl.oz.	240 mL
1 1/2 cup	12 fl.oz.	355 mL
2 cups or 1 pint	16 fl.oz.	475 mL
4 cups or 1 quart	32 fl.oz.	1 L
1 gallon	128 fl.oz.	4 L

Temperatures Equivalents

FAHRENHEIT(F)	CELSIUS(C) APPROXIMATE)
225 °F	107 °C
250 °F	120 ° °C
275 °F	135 °C
300 °F	150 °C
325 °F	160 °C
350 °F	180 °C
375 °F	190 °C
400 °F	205 °C
425 °F	220 °C
450 °F	235 °C
475 °F	245 °C
500 °F	260 °C

Appendix 2 The Dirty Dozen and Clean Fifteen

The Environmental Working Group (EWG) is a nonprofit, nonpartisan organization dedicated to protecting human health and the environment Its mission is to empower people to live healthier lives in a healthier environment. This organization publishes an annual list of the twelve kinds of produce, in sequence, that have the highest amount of pesticide residue-the Dirty Dozen-as well as a list of the fifteen kinds ofproduce that have the least amount of pesticide residue-the Clean Fifteen.

THE DIRTY DOZEN	
The 2016 Dirty Dozen includes the following produce. These are considered among the year's most important produce to buy organic:	
Strawberries	Spinach
Apples	Tomatoes
Nectarines	Bell peppers
Peaches	Cherry tomatoes
Celery	Cucumbers
Grapes	Kale/collard greens
Cherries	Hot peppers
The Dirty Dozen list contains two additional itemskale/collard greens and hot peppers-because they tend to contain trace levels of highly hazardous pesticides.	

THE CLEAN FIFTEEN	
The least critical to buy organically are the Clean Fifteen list. The following are on the 2016 list:	
Avocados	Papayas
Corn	Kiw
Pineapples	Eggplant
Cabbage	Honeydew
Sweet peas	Grapefruit
Onions	Cantaloupe
Asparagus	Cauliflower
Mangos	
Some of the sweet corn sold in the United States are made from genetically engineered (GE) seedstock. Buy organic varieties of these crops to avoid GE produce.	

Appendix 3 Index

ALICIA D. ELIAS

Printed in the USA
CPSIA information can be obtained
at www.ICGtesting.com
LVHW010802021123
762642LV00029B/34